GREAT CHRISTIAN THINKERS

SIMONE WEIL

Stephen Plant

SERIES EDITOR: PETER VARDY

Triumph
Liguori, Missouri

Published by Triumph
An Imprint of Liguori Publications
Liguori, Missouri

Library of Congress Cataloging-in-Publication Data

Plant, Stephen.
    Simone Weil / Stephen Plant. — 1st U.S. ed.
       p.   cm. — (Great Christian thinkers)
    Includes bibliographical references and index.
    ISBN 0-7648-0116-3
    1. Weil, Simone, 1909–1943. 2. Weil, Simone, 1909–1943—Religion. 3. Phi-
losophers—France—Biography. I. Title. II. Series.
B2430.W474P57   1997
230'.092—dc21
[B]   96-52490

Originally published in English by HarperCollinsPublishers Ltd under the title:
Simone Weil by Stephen Plant

First U.S. Edition 1997
01 00 99 98 97   5 4 3 2 1
Printed in the United States of America

For Kirsty,
with friendship and in truth.

Contents

Preface

This book belongs to a series of introductions to theological thinkers. The aim of the series is to introduce some of the most important Christian thinkers to as wide an audience as possible, and in as intelligible a way as possible. It is an aim Simone Weil would have approved of. Though herself highly academically qualified, Weil believed that the questions addressed by theology, philosophy and literature were too important to be confined to those with a high level of formal academic training. She was surely right.

In one of her books, Weil asked a question that should daunt anyone preparing to explore her thought, and even more, anyone setting out to write about it:

Are there many books or articles which leave us with the impression that the author, first before ever beginning to write, and then again before handing the manuscript to the printer, asked himself with any real concern: 'Am I in line with truth?' Are there many readers who, before opening a book, ask themselves with any real concern: 'Am I going to find truth in here?' (THE NEED FOR ROOTS, 249)

It is hoped that this introduction answers Weil's challenge responsibly.

My thanks are offered to Peter Vardy who has edited this book and others in the same series. It is no platitude to say that his encouragement has been essential to the book's inception and completion. My thanks also to Kirsty Smith whose comments on the manuscript were pertinent and sharp, but always kindly given.

STEPHEN PLANT
LENT 1996

Abbreviations

Details of editions cited are given in Suggested Further Reading.

Date Chart

1938 Visit to Solesmes – first mystical experiences	
	1939 Hitler invades Poland – Second World War begins
1940 Weil family travel to Marseilles	
	1940 June – France surrenders
1941 Begins notebooks from which *Gravity and Grace* are taken	
1941 June – meets Fr Perrin. Works for Thibon. Writes most of *Intimations of Christianity among the Ancient Greeks*	1941 The US enters the war
1942 Leaves France. Travels to America via Casablanca. Arrives in London in December	
1943 Writes *The Need for Roots* 15 April, enters Middlesex Hospital 24 August, Weil dies in Ashford, Kent	
	1945 Allied Victory in Europe

Introduction

The Importance of Simone Weil

Introducing someone's writing is always a dubious enterprise when their own words can speak for themselves. It is, in the words of a Buddhist proverb about teachers of religion, like trying to sell water beside a river. Nevertheless, when a writer's thought is as complex and challenging as Simone Weil's, there may be a role for the kind of introduction attempted in this book. Time is precious, and introductions help one decide whether a writer is worth making an effort to understand. An introduction may even assist the understanding of some ideas better than if one wrestled with them alone. Yet, for this book, the only real measure of its failure or success will be the extent to which it encourages a reading of Weil's own writings.

The inclusion of Weil in this series introducing significant Christian thinkers is remarkable for at least two reasons. Firstly, Weil's impact is the more notable because she is a woman. Christianity and Christian theology have not always found it easy to recognize the distinctive contribution that women bring. The late twentieth century has thankfully been witness to a growing recognition of women in church life and Christian thinking. Though she was not occupied with specifically feminist themes, Weil's inclusion as a leading Christian thinker signals the crucial importance of women to Christian theology.

A second remarkable feature of Weil's inclusion in the series is that she is not universally regarded as a *Christian* thinker at all. She was never baptized and never represented the Church or its theology. Some of the beliefs presented in her writings fall outside the boundaries of what most Christians would regard as orthodox Christian faith. Moreover, she concerned herself with subjects upon which Christians had remained largely silent, such as parallels between the gospels and Greek mythology, and the writings of Karl Marx. Weil demonstrates the importance of those who cross the boundaries of Christian thought and the risks of too rigorously excluding those who do not conform to a strict standard of orthodox belief.

Why read Simone Weil? One reason might be the respect others have for her thought and writings. If such commendations are needed then there is no shortage of people ready to offer them. Simone de Beauvoir, the seminal feminist writer and one of Weil's student contemporaries, wrote of being filled with admiration for her intelligence, asceticism, total commitment and sheer courage. The novelist André Gide called her 'the best spiritual writer of this century', while the poet T. S. Eliot said she had a genius akin to the saints. Her spiritual writings deeply impressed Pope John XXIII, while Pope Paul VI counted her one of the three most important influences on his intellectual development. Albert Camus regarded her as the most penetrating and prophetic social and political thinker since Marx. In spite of calling her a 'revolutionary melancholic', Leon Trotsky, who stayed with her in Paris where they argued late into the night, was impressed by her. Finally, Iris Murdoch, philosopher and novelist, regularly cites Weil as a philosophical and literary authority. Of course, she also had her detractors: Charles de Gaulle unceremoniously said of her: 'The woman was mad'!

The opinions of others are important, and the fact that so many men and women of vastly differing views have found Weil worth reading and understanding should be taken seriously. But, ultimately, the opinions expressed by others are not good enough reasons to read Weil. As a teacher she wisely taught her pupils that they should always make up their own minds.

If it is not sufficient to take someone else's word that she is worth reading, perhaps we should read Weil simply because of her breadth of knowledge. She trained primarily in philosophy, but also studied history and wrote essays and articles on a huge range of historical subjects. She wrote on classical Greek philosophy, on the culture of ancient Rome, on medieval France and on Renaissance Florence. She wrote on political subjects too: on Marxist theory, on Hitler and the Nazis and on colonialism. She developed theories on the economy and on how working in a factory should be restructured to make it more effective and more fruitful. As well as philosophical and historical approaches, she used the disciplines of sociology and anthropology to aid reflection on her subjects. And, of course, she wrote about theology as well, where her lack of academic theological training gave her a freshness of approach to many themes done to death by professional theologians. Yet even breadth of knowledge need not be a good thing, if accompanied by shallowness. The expansiveness of Weil's learning, and the extraordinary range of subjects about which she wrote, are worthwhile only if what she has to say is worth attention.

Perhaps she should be read because of her intelligence. When in 1927 the results in the BA in Philosophy were declared at the Sorbonne University in Paris, Weil was top of the lists, with de Beauvoir second. In 1931, out of 107 candidates at the renowned École Normale Supérieure, only 11 passed, and Weil came seventh. She read and spoke German and English fluently, understood Italian and Spanish, was an excellent translator of classical Greek and could read Sanskrit and Tibetan.

But not even her intelligence is good enough reason to devote attention to her thought. She once wrote that a person who celebrates their own intelligence is like a man condemned to imprisonment who shows off the size of his cell. The truth of a life has almost nothing to do with intelligence. In one of her notebooks Weil jotted down the only thing intelligence can really do: 'We know by means of our intelligence that what the intelligence does not comprehend is more real than what it does comprehend' (GG 116).

Neither the recommendation of others, nor the breadth of her learning, nor the sharpness of her intelligence provides sufficient reason to read Simone Weil. It is not even worth reading Simone Weil merely to write an essay or to pass an exam. The only thing that mattered to Weil in her many writings, and the only really good reason for reading this book and books by her, is that what she thinks might be 'true'. In one of her last letters she wrote:

> I have a sort of growing inner certainty that there is within me a deposit of pure gold which must be handed on. Only I become more and more convinced, by experience, and by observing my contemporaries, that there is no one to receive it ... This does not distress me at all. The mine of gold is inexhaustible. (SL 196 FF.)

The purpose of this introduction is to mine the vein of gold her thought contains. It is not Simone Weil who will be the object of this study, but those things about which she thought so deeply and wrote so well.

Fitting all the breadth and profundity of Weil's thought into this slim volume is an impossible task. It is like fitting a reluctant genie into his bottle. In the next chapter, the main events in Weil's short life will be sketched out. This will provide a context in which to consider her writings. More than most thinkers, Weil's life and thought were inextricably intertwined, and so, though the main aim of the book is to explore her thought, her biography is essential to understanding what she wrote. Chapters 2, 3 and 4 present the subjects that are of particular value in Weil's intellectual legacy. In the final chapter, a brief assessment of Weil's life and thought will be offered.

Simone Weil's Life

A Barren Fig Tree?

Simone Weil was haunted by self-doubt but also by a powerful awareness of the love of God. In 1942, the year before her death, Weil summed up her life in a letter to a friend. Comparing herself with the fig tree Jesus cursed while entering Jerusalem because it did not bear any fruit, she wrote:

> I never read the story of the barren fig tree without trembling. I think that it is a portrait of me. In it also, nature was powerless, and yet it was not excused. Christ cursed it ...
>
> It is not that I actually do fear [God's anger]. By a strange twist, the thought of God's anger only arouses love in me. It is the thought of the possible favour of God and his mercy that makes me tremble with a sort of fear.
>
> On the other hand the sense of being like a barren fig tree for Christ tears my heart. (WG 49)

Weil's characterization of her life as barren and fruitless shows her profound lack of self-confidence. Yet, taking the facts of her life at face value, her self-assessment is pitifully accurate. During her life her writings were almost unknown beyond a few close friends. Those of her essays that were published reached small audiences, and her larger essays became known only after her death. The proletarian revolution to which she devoted so much of the energy of her early life never took place. As a factory labourer seeking solidarity with the working classes, she was a poor worker. Her lack of physical stamina meant she was often too exhausted to engage in close friendships with her fellow workers. The injuries that forced her retreat from the Spanish Civil War were caused not by a Fascist bullet or shell, but by the accidental result of her own clumsiness. In the Second World War she yearned for dangerous front line action, but ended up in a London desk job. She lived to see neither the fall of the 'Great Beast' of Nazism, nor the regeneration of France. She longed for love, and lived the life of an outsider.

Simone Weil was born in Paris in 1909. Her only brother, André, was born three years earlier. Weil's father was a doctor in general practice. Her mother, though not trained in medicine because her father would not give his permission, knew almost as much as her husband having worked so closely with him over the years. Both Weil's parents were Jewish, but neither practised their religion. Dr Weil's atheism, a zealous reaction against the piety of his mother, was an important influence on Simone Weil, and had a great bearing on her later anti-Jewish thinking. In a letter written in 1940, Simone Weil explained her feelings towards her Jewish inheritance. If by 'Jew' one means a follower of a particular religion, she wrote, then 'I have never entered a synagogue and I have never witnessed a Jewish religious ceremony'. If one means by 'Jew' a member of a particular race, she continued, then 'I have no reason to suppose that I have any sort of tie, either through my father or my mother, with the people who lived in Palestine two thousand years ago'.

The home in which Simone Weil grew up was loving and secure. During the First World War, her father served as an army doctor and the family followed him in his frequent moves from town to town. One consequence of this was a closeness in the family which accounts to some degree for Weil's comparative difficulty in relating to her peers. Otherwise her childhood was normal, even mundane, down to the detail of the appendix operation she had when three years old.

Simone's brother André had a brilliant mind, and she compared herself unfavourably to him. As an adult she wrote:

The exceptional gifts of my brother, who had a childhood and youth comparable to those of Pascal [the French mathematician and philosopher], brought my own inferiority home to me. (WG 21)

At first she thought that her mediocrity would exclude her from truth. She soon came to believe that even those who are not intellectual geniuses can enter truth if they long for it enough, and if they pay proper attention. This insight, imprinted on her adolescent mind, remained with her vividly throughout her life.

By the time she had arrived in her mid-teens, Weil had already decided to choose philosophy rather than mathematics as her future academic speciality. At sixteen she enrolled at the prestigious Lycée Henri IV where she studied French, English, History and Philosophy. Her physical appearance at this age changed little during the rest of her life. One of her fellow students, her friend Simone Pétrement, described Weil's distinctive appearance:

[She had a] small, thin face, which seemed to be devoured by her hair and glasses. A fine-boned delicate nose, dark eyes that looked out boldly, a neck that strained forward and gave the impression of a burning, almost indiscreet curiosity; but her full mouth gave one a feeling of sweetness and good nature. Looking at them carefully her features do not lack charm and even beauty; it was a face at once insolent and tender, bold in asking questions but with a timid smile that seemed to mock itself ... Her charm remained hidden from most people, who saw in Simone only a totally intellectual being. Her body was thin, her gestures lively but also clumsy. She wore clothes with a masculine cut, always the same outfit (a kind of suit with a very wide skirt and a long, narrow jacket), and always flat-heeled shoes. (SIMONE PÉTREMENT, *SIMONE WEIL: A LIFE*, 11–12)

3

Weil's philosophy teacher at the Lycée was the celebrated Emile Chartier, better known as 'Alain'. From him Weil learned how to express her ideas clearly and succinctly. He also taught her to respect the Greek philosopher Plato (427–347 BC), and reinforced her childhood love of geometry. At the end of her two years at the school she won the philosophy prize. Alain's final comment on his star pupil was characteristically perceptive. He noted that she was

... an excellent pupil; a rare strength of mind, wide culture. Will succeed brilliantly if she does not embark on obscure paths. In any case she will attract attention. (PÉTREMENT 41)

In 1927, although she was placed first in examinations for the philosophy degree at the Sorbonne, she failed the highly competitive entrance exams for the École Normale Supérieure, and was forced to study more widely before passing them a year later. Affiliated to the Sorbonne, the École Normale was one of the most respected academic institutions in France, giving its graduates access to teaching posts in France's best schools. Weil studied there from 1928 to 1931, and entered fully into student life. She even joined a rugby team. In 1930, following an attack of viral sinusitis, Weil began experiencing migraine headaches. These were to afflict her with regular and excruciating ferocity for the rest of her life – a fact that should be borne in mind when examining the theme of affliction in Chapter 3. In July 1931, Weil qualified as a teacher and presented an extended dissertation on 'Science and Perception' in the work of the French philosopher René Descartes (1596–1650).

To recount Weil's student days in terms of her academic studies alone, however, is to tell only half the story. The years in Paris from 1925 to 1931 were also for Weil years in which she was deeply engaged in political reflection and action. These were eventful times as the political parties and organizations of the Left battled with one another. Weil was painfully aware of the debilitating effects of the splits in Trade Unions and political parties represent-ing the interests of working people, and she toiled with little suc-cess for unity. In America, the Wall Street Crash shattered the illusion of world-wide economic prosperity. The repercussions were felt in France, where working people faced high unemploy-ment and worsening working conditions. In 1927, Weil had worked long hours on a farm in Normandy bringing in the har-vest. When she returned to Paris she began a Social Education Group with friends, giving free lessons in philosophy to factory and railway workers.

In this rapidly changing social environment, and with a per-sonal conviction informed by her conversations with rural and industrial workers, Weil became ever more involved with politics. When a petition was drawn up campaigning against the compul-sory military instruction given to male students at the École, she was vigorous in gathering signatures to make the training volun-tary. She pestered one of her lecturers, M. Bouglé, for a donation to a fund for the unemployed. When the time came for the authori-ties to place her in a school, she asked to be placed in an industrial centre. Instead, with malicious intent, they posted her to Le Puy, a relatively quiet non-industrial town in south-eastern France. Bouglé, who had a hand in the decision, is reputed to have said: 'We shall send the Red Virgin as far away as possible so that we shall never hear of her again.'

From 1931 to 1934 Simone Weil was a teacher of Philosophy. Her students liked her and in return she took a genuine interest in them. In a letter to a former student Weil asked if there was 'still the same good spirit of comradeship' amongst a class that she had taught. Her teaching methods, however, were somewhat unorthodox. She was less interested in her students passing exams than inspiring them with her love of philosophy. From a student's notes, it seems that what she actually taught was a brief history of Western thought. She explored basic philosophical questions like 'How do we perceive the world?' and 'How does language affect the way we come to grips with the world?'. She also taught the basics of ethics, sociology and political science (these lectures are published as *Lectures in Philosophy*). To those who struggled with what they learned, she taught extra classes free of charge.

If her unconventional teaching practices prejudiced the school authorities against her, then her activities outside school made things even worse. From the point of view of her employers, Weil's life was inappropriate for a professional person. She disdained spending money on clothes or luxuries, buying books instead, and giving the rest of her salary to workers' strike funds. She refused to have the heating on in her room because, she believed, the unemployed had to live in the cold, and therefore she should too. In her support for the poor and unemployed of Le Puy she was untiring. She was also prominent in political demonstrations of various kinds and her name appeared in the local papers as a result. Once, she led a delegation to the local Mayor to ask for a rise in unemployment benefit. This kind of behaviour in a schoolteacher, employed by the state, was frowned upon. In consequence, the authorities moved her three times in as many years, passing her like a bad penny from Le Puy to Auxerre (1932), and from Auxerre to Roanne (1933). She taught her classes diligently but beyond the school gates she continued to meet local workers, to teach them in her spare time and to campaign for better conditions for workers and the unemployed.

Somehow, Weil also found time and energy to think and to write. In 1932, she spent six weeks in Germany and saw the conflict between the Communists and the National Socialists at first-hand. Weil wrote several essays about her experiences. Her socialist friends were optimistic that a working class revolution in Germany was imminent. Weil, however, believed that in spite of the heroism of individuals, the working classes were too disunited to achieve anything. Weil saw immediately that the Nazis were evil, but she also saw striking resemblances between National Socialism and Communism. When published, these essays estranged her from many of her former friends. Weil's fully developed political theories are found in *Oppression and Liberty*, a collection of essays published after her death. Some of the ways Weil sought to develop new political and social theories are outlined in Chapter 4 of this book.

By 1934, Weil had become convinced that the reason socialist leaders were so out of touch with working people was that none of them knew what it was like to work in a factory. She therefore obtained permission from the Ministry of Education to take a one-year 'sabbatical' for 'personal studies'. She was granted unpaid leave and, after a break to finish writing *Oppression and Liberty*, on 4 December she began work as a factory hand in the Alsthom factory in Paris.

She worked at Alsthom for four months, after which she needed a period of convalescence in Switzerland to recover. In April 1935 she was back at work, this time at the Carnaud factory. In June she was working at the Renault plant. The journal Weil kept throughout her 'sabbatical', though dispassionately descriptive, records a painfully difficult year for her. It was, nevertheless, a year which led her in several new and fruitful directions. She had learned a great deal about living with affliction, and her high regard for manual labour remained undiminished. But the year had also, in her own words, left her 'in pieces, soul and body'.

During her summer holidays, Weil travelled in Spain and Portugal with her parents. In Portugal, on a solitary day's outing, she entered a small fishing village on the evening of a religious festival. The candle-light procession, and the hymns of 'heart-rending sadness' reached deep into her exhausted soul. Later, she wrote:

... the conviction was suddenly borne in upon me that Christianity is pre-eminently the religion of slaves, that slaves cannot help belonging to it, and I among others. (WG 24)

In October 1936, now aged twenty-seven, she was back teaching Philosophy, this time at Bourges. She entered into a long correspondence with Monsieur Bernard, a factory manager, making various suggestions to him on how to run a factory. She also wrote a series of articles for his factory magazine introducing some of the classics of ancient Greek poetry and drama: for example on Homer's *Iliad*, and on Sophocles' *Antigone*. This was in keeping with the desire she had as a student to educate the working classes. It was also because she believed that the tragic themes of the classic dramas were more readily understood by people rooted in the ordinary world than by stuffy academic scholars. She also corresponded with Bernard in June 1936 when 'sit-in' strikes broke out across France. Unsurprisingly, Bernard did not share Weil's joy at seeing workers in control of whole factories.

In August of the same year, Weil's hunger for a cause led her to Spain, where civil war had erupted between Fascists and a loose coalition of communists, socialists and anti-Fascists. Weil had always been a pacifist. In this instance, however, because she hoped so fervently for the victory of the anti-Fascists, she believed she was morally involved in the conflict. It was not her way to stay on the sidelines. She travelled to Barcelona where she enrolled on the anti-Fascist side as a member of the Anarchist Militia. She volunteered for the most dangerous missions, but her inexperience and innate clumsiness made her a liability. On 20 August 1936, she fell into a pot of boiling cooking fat, and her war was over. By the end of September she was back in France.

To begin with, she intended to return to Spain, but the 'smell of blood and terror' associated with civil war disillusioned her greatly. While in Spain, Weil had almost witnessed the execution of a priest by her own militia unit and had considered intervening on his behalf. On another occasion during her time at the Spanish front, a fifteen-year-old youth had been captured by the anarchists during a skirmish. He was told he could either change sides or die. After a day to think about it, the boy said he did not want to change sides and was promptly shot. This execution, and other instances of brutality by her own side, lay heavily on Weil's conscience.

After convalescing in Italy and Switzerland, Weil returned briefly to teaching, though with frequent periods of sick-leave. In 1937 and 1938, Weil's life took a dramatic turn. Though she had considered God as a topic for philosophy, she had until then remained an agnostic. Her experiences as a factory worker and her brief service in the Spanish Civil War caused her to reflect deeply on religion. This left her open to several profound spiritual encounters with Christianity. During a visit to Assisi in 1937, something stronger than her own will compelled her for the first time to go down on her knees in prayer. A year later she spent Holy Week at the Benedictine monastery of Solesmes:

> *I was suffering from splitting headaches; each sound hurt me like a blow; by an extreme effort of concentration I was able to rise above this wretched flesh, to leave it to suffer by itself, heaped up in a corner, and to find a pure and perfect joy in the unimaginable beauty of the chanting and the words. This experience enabled me by analogy to get a better understanding of the possibility of loving divine love in the midst of affliction.* (WG 24)

A young English Catholic led her to reflect upon the religious power of the sacraments. He introduced her to a poem by George Herbert, a sixteenth-century English poet, on the love of God.

> *Love bade me welcome; yet my soul drew back,*
> *   Guilty of dust and sin.*
> *But quick-ey'd Love, observing me grow slack*
> *   From my first entrance in,*
> *Drew nearer to me, sweetly questioning*
> *   If I lack'd any thing.*

'A guest', I answer'd, 'worthy to be here.'
  Love said, 'You shall be he.'
'I the unkind, ungrateful? Ah my dear,
  I cannot look on thee.'
Love took my hand, and smiling did reply,
  'Who made the eyes but I?'

'Truth Lord, but I have marr'd them; let my shame
  Go where it doth deserve.'
'And know you not', says Love, 'who bore the blame?'
  'My dear, then I will serve.'
'You must sit down', says Love, ' and taste my meat.'
  So I did sit and eat.

She learned it by heart and would recite it to herself when the pain of her headaches was at its worst. She later wrote: 'It was during one of these recitations that, as I told you, Christ himself came down and took possession of me' (WG 25). These mystical experiences effected a redirection of her thought towards religious and theological themes.

In 1939, the world's drift towards war preoccupied Weil increasingly. She continued to write on classical Greek literature. On the eve of war she wrote about Homer's *Iliad*, but now drew out of this poem the cold brutality of violence, and the ways in which the human spirit can resist it. When, in March, German troops entered Prague, she finally renounced pacifism. She drew parallels between Nazi Germany and ancient Rome at the height of its powers. Hitler, she argued, was the only leader in two thousand years who had learned to copy the Romans. Not only did the Romans believe themselves to be a superior race, they were also completely ruthless in their domination of other cities and cultures. Her antipathy towards the Nazis proved well-founded when in September the Germans invaded Poland and world war broke out.

In 1940, Weil began to read Hindu Scriptures, particularly the *Bhagavadgita*. For Weil, this classic text did not contradict but complemented Christianity. The way in which Weil arrived at this conclusion is explored in the next chapter.

With the outbreak of war, and lacking the pacifist convictions that would once have conditioned her response, Weil struggled to find the best way to fight against the Nazis. Characteristically, she sought out a means to serve which would involve sharing the worst kinds of personal risk. She conceived a plan for front line nurses, a plan she continued to advocate energetically throughout the remainder of her life. Her idea was to form a mobile unit of female nurses available to give first-aid at the most dangerous parts of the front line of battle. She believed that it would have a moral effect on enemy and friend alike:

> *The mere persistence of a few humane services in the very centre of the battle, the climax of inhumanity, would be a signal defiance of the inhumanity which the enemy has chosen for himself and which he compels us also to practise.* (SL 144–5)

Though her plan aroused interest with the French authorities, it never came to fruition.

In June 1940, France surrendered to the German Army. Northern France, including Paris where the Weil family lived, was occupied by the Germans. Southern France, however, remained nominally independent, but with a Government based in Vichy that was sympathetic to the Nazis. As a family with Jewish ancestry, the Weils believed that their safety might be jeopardized if they stayed in occupied France. Thus, on the day the Germans were marching along one road into Paris, the Weils were leaving by another for Vichy France.

The Weil family travelled to Marseilles in September 1940. Marseilles was the chief seaport of France, with a thriving cosmopolitan life. As she discovered more about the region in which

Marseilles was situated, however, it was its history which capti-
vated Weil. Between the eleventh and thirteenth centuries the
region had been politically and culturally independent of the rest
of France. It was defined by a distinct language which gave the
region its name, the Languedoc. The region had also been clearly
defined by its distinctive religion, Catharism, whose adherents in
the Languedoc were known as the Albigensians. This religion was
a heretical descendant of the early Christian Church, and its
followers believed life to be dominated by the conflict between
the forces of good and evil. Jesus was regarded as a rebel against
the cruelty of the Old Testament God. In 1208 a crusade was
launched against the Albigensians by the Roman Catholic Church
which killed thousands of people with merciless cruelty. Weil felt a
strong sympathy for the beliefs of the Albigensians, especially for
their rejection of the God of the Old Testament which, as we shall
see in the first part of the next chapter, was a consistent feature of
her own thought. Weil recognized that it was impossible to be a
follower of a religion that had been dead for centuries. Nevertheless, during her two years in the region she studied its now dead
language, its history and religion in depth. This study left indelible
imprints on her developing theology. Several articles arising out of
this study and her ongoing study of other religious and philosophical traditions, were published in the journal *Cahiers du Sud*.

Weil did not, however, only bury her head in books, she also
made efforts to establish personal contacts in the area. In the
Cahiers du Sud she wrote very positively about meetings of the
Young Christian Workers' Movement which she attended. In
these meetings her old involvement in workers' movements, and
her developing religious interests, were brought together. Among
these young Christians, she wrote, 'Christianity has an authentic
ring; it is that which used to give to slaves a supernatural liberty'.

Early on in Marseilles, Weil was put in touch with a Resistance
group. After she had been involved only a short time, however, an
informer betrayed the group, and the police came calling at the

Weil family flat. She was subsequently examined by a military magistrate on several occasions, but, in spite of his threats and attempt to intimidate her by threatening her parents, she said nothing and was released. She re-established links with the Resistance during her last months in Marseilles. This time round, she was more effective. She maintained links between different members of the Marseilles Resistance, acting as a courier for messages. She also distributed copies of the movement's anti-Fascist journal.

As important as any of her other contacts, however, was her increasing contact with practising Roman Catholics. In Marseilles her attitude towards Christianity and the institutional Church began to become fixed. Weil's relationship to Christianity was ambivalent – but it was firmly ambivalent. She regarded herself as a Christian, but felt that she could not be baptized and join the Church. She never wavered from the opinions she developed in Marseilles.

In Marseilles, Weil met a Catholic priest whose intelligence and integrity she considered uniquely qualified him to be the conversation partner she needed to work through her questions about the Christian faith. Father Perrin was a priest at the Dominican Convent in Marseilles. Weil was introduced to him in June 1941 and when he was moved to Montpellier in March 1942 they kept in touch, meeting and writing to each other until Weil left France. It was with Perrin above all that Weil worked through her hesitations about baptism. It was also for Perrin that she wrote her 'Spiritual Autobiography' (WG 19–36), to which reference has already been made, and which gives an account of her evolving experience of God. The conclusion Weil drew from her conversations with Father Perrin was that though she regarded herself as a Christian she could not be baptized into a church that professed so many beliefs with which she could not in conscience agree. In spite of this, she later advised her brother to have his daughter baptized, and when ill in London she hinted to a friend that if she became comatose, the friend should arrange for her to be baptized.

In spite of these apparent contradictions in Weil's attitude towards baptism into the Roman Catholic Church, the simple truth is that she never was baptized.

In August 1941 Perrin put her in touch with a devout Catholic layman, Gustave Thibon, who was a vine farmer in St-Marcel d'Ardéche on the river Rhône. She worked for him throughout the vine harvest. Although Thibon offered her accommodation in his home, she insisted on living in a dilapidated cottage nearby. The work was back-breaking and the working day was long. Weil learned the 'Our Father' in its original Greek, and recited it each morning before work and whenever the work and her migraines became too much to bear. Sometimes during these recitations she would feel Christ present with her, 'his presence ... infinitely more real, more moving, more clear than on that first occasion when he took possession of me' (WG 28).

The tendency towards an ascetic lifestyle had always been a feature of Weil's character. During her time in Marseilles, however, this tendency began to become obsessive. A new friend, a ship's doctor named Bercher was worried by this. He later noted to Father Perrin that to Simone, eating seemed a base and disgusting function. He told her that his sister, a Benedictine nun, once recounted the story of a nun who went for a long time without eating, nourishing herself on the eucharist alone. Weil found this story quite reasonable. In Marseilles, Weil would not queue for rations, and often gave her own rations in packages to the prison camps where the enemies of the Nazis were being gathered by the puppet Vichy Government.

After two years, but what must have seemed a lifetime, the Weil family were given permission to leave France. The period in Vichy France had been immensely productive for Weil. Between 1940 and 1942 Weil had written most of the essays subsequently published in *Intimations of Christianity among the Ancient Greeks*, she had filled the notebooks from which *Gravity and Grace* was extracted, and had written intelligently about the Languedoc, its literature and its religion. Before her departure, as though she knew she was bidding farewell to her friends for the last time, she gave her precious notebooks to Gustave Thibon, and her 'Spiritual Autobiography' to Father Perrin. The Weil family went by ship to Casablanca in May, where they were detained in a holding camp. She watched with interest the religious practices of the Jews there. After a brief wait, the family boarded a ship for America, where they arrived on 6 July 1942.

In New York Weil continued to pester local priests about her inner dialogue concerning baptism, writing the 'Letter to a Priest' (in *Gateway to God*) which elaborated on what she had told Perrin about her doubts. Above all, Weil was desperate to gain permission to go to London to join the Free French forces. She wanted especially to gain acceptance of her plan for front line nurses. In the French Consulate in New York she met an old acquaintance, Simone Deitz, and together they explored New York, attending black churches in Harlem on Sundays. In November, having finally received the necessary permission, the two Simones began the hazardous two-week journey to Britain.

Because of her former communist links, it took longer than was usual for Weil to pass through the holding camp for refugees which sought to weed out potential threats to national security. An old student contemporary, Maurice Schumann (later Foreign Minister in de Gaulle's Government), was, fortuitously, a senior figure in the Free French Resistance. Schumann facilitated Weil's induction into London life and into the ranks of those working for the liberation of France. She took lodgings in Holland Park, west London, with a widow and her two children, whom she enjoyed assisting with their homework. Weil's letters to her parents show how much she enjoyed London, and liked its people:

In the evenings people dance in the open air in the parks. The more frivolous little cockney girls go every evening to the parks and the pubs with boys whom they pick up on the way – to the great distress of their mothers, who cannot persuade them to go to church instead.
(SL 199)

The indomitable humour of the British in adversity matched what she had heard of it, and she savoured the vibrant atmosphere of pub culture. Nevertheless, Weil was in London for other reasons than to enjoy herself. She continued to work at her theological studies, sleeping only a few hours a night. Her landlady worried because she ate so little, but Weil complained that she could not eat while those in occupied France were dying of hunger.

Schumann found work for her at the provisional Government's Ministry of the Interior in the Commissariat of action upon France. Here, her superior, Closon, gave her the job of reporting on all documents coming out of France of a political nature. Weil read and summarized reports produced by Resistance groups about the political shape of post-war France. She was well-suited for the task, but her heart was not in it. She continued to press her idea for front line nurses, but de Gaulle rejected it. Another idea of Weil's, however, he accepted. She suggested that a 'Supreme Council of the Revolt' be established in France to co-ordinate from within the movement to liberate the continent. Weil also asked to be parachuted into occupied France as a French agent. Her health, physical and mental, made this impossible, as did her obviously Jewish appearance, but Weil could not see this. When her friend Simone Deitz was accepted for such a mission, Weil pressed her to swap places. When Deitz refused the exchange, Weil was beside herself with jealousy and only relaxed after the mission was cancelled.

It was as part of her work in the Ministry of the Interior that Weil was asked to give attention to a philosophical basis for a post-war French Constitution. This led to her essays 'On Human

Personality', 'Draft for a Statement of Human Obligations', and the book-length *The Need for Roots*. In these essays, Weil explored how conditions for a post-war society in Europe (though particularly in France) might be established. It was not sufficient, Weil believed, to expel the Nazi Germans if what replaced them was to be nothing more than a French version of the same totalitarian ideology. The vision which she developed will be addressed in greater depth in Chapter 4.

Writing reports, however, was not the dangerous mission that Weil longed for. She bitterly regretted her decision to leave Vichy France, where, she now believed, the chances of serving her country were better. Overwork, hunger and despondency eventually took their toll, and in April 1943 Deitz found her prostrate with weakness in her lodgings. She was admitted to the Middlesex Hospital. Her doctor diagnosed tuberculosis, but Weil stubbornly refused treatment. She also refused to eat more than small quantities of food, repeating to medical staff what she had told her landlady, that she could not eat more food than those in occupied France. She was not short of visitors, but she was not always pleased to see them. She argued with Schumann and Closon, her Free French superiors, because they would not agree to send her into France. Also, she was increasingly frustrated with the myopia of the Free French authorities, who were intent only on winning the war without any thought about what should happen afterwards. She resigned from the Free French in July.

Her condition was not in itself life-threatening, but because she was by now habituated to tiny quantities of food, it hurt her to over-fill her stomach, and she was not able to take in sufficient calories to strengthen her body. Eventually, the medical staff at the hospital, impatient with her, and short of beds, insisted that she be moved, and a place was found for her at the Grosvenor Sanatorium in Ashford, Kent. By now she was very weak indeed, though her last letter to her parents was the first of her regular correspondence to give them any indication that she was ill:

Darlings,
Very little time or inspiration for letters now. They will be short,
erratic, and far between. But you have another source of consolation
[a new granddaughter] ... Au revoir, darlings, Heaps and heaps of love.
(SL 201)

Weil was taken to Ashford by Mme Closon, the wife of her forgiving former superior. From her new room she could look out over the Kent fields towards France. Again, she struggled with her doctors, and refused to eat. Eventually she was unable to move at all, and she died on 24 August 1943. Three days later the Coroner recorded that she had died of

... cardiac failure due to myocardial and pulmonary tuberculosis. The
deceased did kill and slay herself by refusing to eat whilst the balance
of her mind was disturbed.

The implication that she had committed suicide made her of momentary interest to the local press. One ran a story headed: 'French Professor starves herself to death'. Another carried the headline: 'Death from starvation, French Professor's curious sacrifice'. Did Simone Weil starve herself to death? Those who knew her best think the answer is no. Weil had never been a big eater, and years of privation meant that by 1943 it caused her agonizing pain to force food into her shrunken stomach. Also, Weil really believed that in some strange way her refusal to eat benefited those who were hungry in France. She knew, of course, that the food she did not eat would not be sent to France, but she believed her lack of excess was an act of spiritual sacrifice which mattered. Ultimately, the question about whether Weil's death was wilfully self-inflicted is best judged in the light of her writings, with their unique and enigmatic blend of celebration of life and self-denial.

Seven people attended her funeral. Among them were her landlady, M. and Mme Closon, Simone Deitz and Maurice Schumann.

In an ironic twist, the priest who had been asked to come missed his train and Schumann took the missal and read the funeral prayers. Weil's landlady threw a bouquet into the grave tied with a tricolour ribbon.

Difficulties in Reading Weil's Writings

Before entering into a more detailed account of Weil's thought, a few remarks about the nature of her writings and the difficulties associated in reading them are necessary.

The first problem with her writings is that during her short life her interests and beliefs changed and developed. Her early immersion in classical philosophy and political theory gave way to an increasing interest in the study of religions and in theology. Nevertheless, as we have already seen, she continued to write about philosophy and politics until her death. One way to make the developments in her thought clear would be to examine her thought in chronological sequence. However, this is not the approach taken here. Instead, her ideas have been grouped into themes, for example dealing in Chapter 4 with her political theory, even though some of her political writings were written earlier, and others later, in her life.

A second difficulty when reading Weil's writings and struggling to understand her ideas is that much of what she wrote was put into notebooks. These are condensed and pithy observations which she intended, but rarely had the chance, to develop more fully later on. Because she did not, through force of circumstances beyond her control, publish more than a fraction of what she wrote, these notebooks were the place where she worked out her ideas. Reading the volumes of her notebooks one finds her circling round the same subject again and again, like a seagull looking for food, approaching the same subject from different angles. It is also in the nature of notes that they are not intended to be final statements of belief, but sometimes merely a getting on to paper of an undeveloped thought. Consequently, Weil occasionally seems to write two statements which directly contradict one another. One person who tried to solve such difficulties was Gustave Thibon, the host and friend for whom Weil picked grapes in 1941. Thibon edited the notebooks Weil left with him in May 1942. From three volumes in French, he arranged passages into themes, such as 'Gravity and Grace', 'Void and Compensation', 'Detachment', etc. This edited collection is now available in English as the book *Gravity and Grace*. Though this book is an excellent place to start reading Weil, it is not the notebooks in their original form, but the notebooks edited by a Roman Catholic layman. As a reader, this fact too is worth bearing in mind.

While it is useful to be aware of the difficulties of reading Simone Weil, they should not be taken as grounds to despair of ever understanding her. When she is not condensing her thought into notes, but writing letters or introductions to classical Greek literature for workers' journals, or even articles for academic periodicals, Weil is a gifted communicator who writes logically and clearly.

A third difficulty in reading Weil's writings concerns the 'mystical' dimension of Weil's thought. What is mysticism? In daily conversation the word 'mystic' is sometimes used to describe a person with strange psychic powers. When speaking about religious experience however, 'mystical' has a very serious if specialized meaning. A mystical experience is one which has a divine or sacred significance that surpasses natural human apprehension. Religious mystics who have encountered God beyond the sphere of natural human apprehension find it difficult to put their experiences into words. Weil's writings are often mystical in this specialized sense. Where she struggles to express mystical experiences of Christ in words Weil is difficult to understand – not because she is confused, but because mysticism, like fine art or poetry, is meant to be experienced, not subjected to rational analysis.

There are two ways in which mysticism shows through in Weil's writings. Firstly, in Weil's writings on, for example, the love of God and affliction, or on the experience of work, it becomes clear that behind her theological reflections is a personal mystical experience of affliction, or of work, which fuels her thinking. A second way in which mysticism is present in Weil's writings are the very rare, but important passages, where she departs from the rules of philosophy and theology, and writes in an imaginative mystical style. The most striking of these is a passage written either during her last months in Paris, or perhaps when she was living in Marseilles. This passage communicates more effectively than this chapter is able to Weil's experience of God in Christ, and of the way she responded to God.

He entered my room and said: 'Poor creature, you who understand nothing, who know nothing. Come with me and I will teach you things which you do not suspect.' I followed him.

He took me into a church. It was new and ugly. He led me up to the altar and said: 'Kneel down.' I said 'I have not been baptized.' He said: 'Fall on your knees before this place, in love, as before the place where lies the truth.' I obeyed.

He brought me out and made me climb up to a garret. Through the open window one could see the whole city spread out, some wooden scaffolding, and the river on which boats were being unloaded. The garret was empty, except for a table and two chairs. He bade me be seated.

We were alone. He spoke. From time to time someone would enter, mingle in the conversation, then leave again.

Winter had gone; spring had not yet come. The branches of the trees lay bare, without buds, in the cold air full of sunshine.

The light of day would arise, shine forth in splendour, and fade away; then the moon and the stars would enter through the window. And then once more the dawn would come up.

At times he would fall silent, take some bread from a cupboard, and we would share it. This bread really had the taste of bread. I have never found that taste again.

He would pour out some wine for me, and some for himself – wine which tasted of the sun and of the soil upon which this city was built.

At other times we would stretch ourselves out on the floor of the garret, and sweet sleep would enfold me. Then I would wake and drink in the light of the sun.

He had promised to teach me, but he did not teach me anything. We talked about all kinds of things, in a desultory way, as do old friends.

One day he said to me: 'Now go.' I fell down before him, I clasped his knees, I implored him not to drive me away. But he threw me out on the stairs. I went down unconscious of anything, my heart as it were in shreds. I wandered along the streets. Then I realized that I had no idea where his house lay.

I have never tried to find it again. I understood that he had come for me by mistake. My place is not in that garret. It can be anywhere – in a prison cell, in one of those middle-class drawing rooms full of knick-knacks and red plush, in the waiting-room of a station – anywhere, except in that garret.

Sometimes I cannot help trying, fearfully and remorsefully, to repeat to myself a part of what he said to me. How am I to know if I remember rightly? He is not there to tell me.

I know well that he does not love me. How could he love me? And yet deep down within me something, a particle of myself, cannot help thinking, with fear and trembling, that perhaps, in spite of all, he loves me. (QUOTED DAVID MCLELLAN, *SIMONE WEIL: UTOPIAN PESSIMIST*, MACMILLAN, XIII–XIV)

2

Weil's Understanding of God

From her correspondence with Father Perrin it is clear Simone Weil believed – accurately or not – that she had always been a Christian. It was not the experiences in Portugal, Assisi or Solesmes which were her first contacts with Christianity; Weil believed that in some sense she had been *born* into it:

> *I always adopted the Christian attitude as the only possible one. I might say that I was born, I grew up and I always remained within the Christian inspiration.* (WG 20)

> *From my earliest childhood I always had also the Christian idea of love for one's neighbour, to which I gave the name of justice.* (WG 22)

However, Weil's understanding of God and of what it means to live within the 'Christian inspiration' diverged greatly from what was acceptable to a priest like Perrin. To Weil, many traditional features of Christian belief seemed irrelevant or fruitless. The existence or non-existence of God, she believed as a student, was an insoluble philosophical problem. She had no concern with salvation or the afterlife, believing it to be a distraction from this life. Indeed to Weil, the Church's system of religious belief (its 'dogma'), was an unnecessary addition to the essential Christian message:

> *Of course I knew quite well that my conception of life was Christian. That is why it never occurred to me that I could enter the Christian*

community. I had the idea that I was born inside. But to add dogma to this conception of life, without being forced to do so by indisputable evidence, would have seemed to me a lack of honesty. (WG 22)

One of Weil's main reasons for refusing baptism which in other respects she so desired was precisely the way in which the orthodox dogma of the Church is so exclusive. To Weil, the institutional Church, historically, had abused its authority to expel those who disagreed with its interpretation of Christian belief. The phrase used formally to excommunicate from the Church was *anathema sit*. Weil notes:

It is the use of these two little words anathema sit. *It is not their existence, but the way they have been employed up till now. It is that also which prevents me from crossing the threshold of the Church.* (WG 32)

In spite of this, when another priest in Marseilles challenged this attitude to dogma and said, not unkindly, that she was a heretic, Weil was flabbergasted.

Sources for Our Knowledge of God

If Weil did not shape her theological convictions according to the strict orthodoxy of the Roman Catholic Church, what were the sources of her belief? Weil believed throughout her life that the truth about God was not limited to one religion. On the contrary, she noted that:

It is impossible that the whole truth should not be present at every time and every place, available for anyone who desires it. 'Whoever asks for bread'. Truth is bread. It is absurd to suppose that for centuries nobody, or hardly anybody, desired the truth, and then that in the following centuries it was desired by whole peoples. (FLN 302)

God's truth did not first enter the world with Christ, nor has it since been available since Jesus' incarnation only to Church members. Weil thought that many religious traditions, though they differed in outward appearance, agreed with the Christian gospels in other fundamental respects:

> *Except in countries that have subordinated their spiritual life to imperialism, a mystic doctrine lies at the secret core of every religion; and although the mystic doctrines differ from each other, they are not only similar but absolutely identical as regards a certain number of essential points.* (OL 176)

The most obvious non-Christian source of religious truth to Weil was the philosophy and literature of the ancient Greeks. Weil believed that Homer's *Iliad* and the tragedies of the playwrights Aeschylus (525–456 BC) and Sophocles (*c.*496–406 BC) 'bear the clearest indication that the poets who produced them were in a state of holiness' (NR 224). Not only were they works of genius, Weil believed they contained divine truth. In the essays of *Intimations of Christianity among the Ancient Greeks*, Weil surveyed the jewels of Ancient Greek literature. In Homer's *Iliad*, for example, she perceived a 'miraculous object ... the only veritable epic of the Western world' (IC 51).

It is, however, the repeated interaction between Greek thought and Christian theology in the essays that is their most striking feature. Weil believed that connections could be made between Christianity and the classics of ancient Greek poetry. Weil was not the first Christian thinker to make such a link. In the third century, for example, Clement of Alexandria wrote that 'philosophy was given to the Greeks to fit their ears for the good news'. St Clement believed that Greek philosophy had value as a preparation for the Christian gospel. Weil's position was quite different. Greek thought did not, for her, pave the way to Christianity; rather it contained within it essential truths also contained in the gospels.

One example, taken from many possible instances in Weil's essays, illustrates the seriousness of her suggestion. It concerns the Greek myth of Prometheus, which was told most beautifully by Aeschylus in the play *Prometheus Bound*. Prometheus belonged to the Titans, a race of semi-divine beings, descended from the gods. Prometheus stole fire from heaven and, because of his selfless love for them, gave it to humankind. For this crime Zeus, the chief of the gods, chained Prometheus to a rock where an eagle came daily to feast on his liver, which grew back at night, until he was eventually freed.

'If one compares lines from the *Prometheus*,' wrote Weil, 'the similarity of the story of Prometheus with that of Christ appears with blinding evidence' (IC 58). Firstly, she suggested, like Christ, Prometheus suffered because of his love for humanity. Crying in agony to heaven Prometheus shouts:

I have delivered mortals
from the damnation that would have flung them into Hades.
It is for this fault that these tortures crush me. (IC 62)

As Christ was crucified for love of humanity, so Prometheus was *crucified* (and Weil uses exactly this word) upon the rock for the same reason.

Aeschylus also describes Prometheus as being, like Christ, the instructor of human beings who has taught them all things necessary for their salvation. Indeed, Prometheus describes his suffering with the Greek word *pascho*, from which the French word for the Passion (suffering) of Christ is taken. In crucifying Prometheus, Weil continued, Zeus opened the way of wisdom to humanity, for it is only through an understanding of suffering that a true knowledge of God is possible.

In addition to the parallels between the suffering of Prometheus and Christ, and their origin in love for humanity, Weil makes another observation concerning the relationship of Zeus to

Prometheus and God to Christ. Contrary to what the horror of the punishment might lead one to believe, there was, she suggested, a high degree of consent and co-operation between Zeus and Prometheus, and their relationship mirrors that between God and Christ. In Aeschylus' play, Zeus and Prometheus are said to be one. The crucifixion of Prometheus is Zeus' chosen way to give an understanding of suffering to humanity. From his rock, Prometheus says that Zeus

> ... shall soften one day, when
> as I have said, he shall be shattered; he, the inflexible,
> he shall appease his anger; in union with me and in friendship
> he shall hasten to me as I hasten to him. (IC 62)

In some versions of the myth, Prometheus' case is so compelling that Zeus is eventually forced to unchain him. Weil concluded that in some mysterious way Prometheus is a part of Zeus himself, crucified on the rock. This idea, the separation of God from himself, only makes sense, Weil suggested, when it is recalled that Christ on his cross cried out that he had been abandoned by God (Matthew 27:46). At the moment of crucifixion, there is an apparent opposition between Father and Son, just as there is between Zeus and Prometheus. Paradoxically, in the stories of Prometheus and of Christ's crucifixion, there is a moment when God is both executioner and victim, slave and master. This interpretation is reinforced when Prometheus freely acknowledges that he has accepted affliction for the sake of humanity: 'I knew all that, I consented, I have consented to take the blame' (IC 70).

In one respect, Weil acknowledged a difference between the crucifixion of Prometheus and Christ. Prometheus' sacrifice, she argued, 'never appears as a historical dated fact which might have happened at a certain point in time and at a certain place' (IC 70). Naturally, the historical events of the life and death of Jesus cannot have been known centuries earlier by Aeschylus. Thus, Weil believed, there is nothing in the comparison of these two stories that weakens in any way the distinctive historical truth of the gospels. However, if Christ existed before the foundation of the world as the Lamb that was slain (Revelation 13:8), then, Weil wrote: 'The story of Prometheus is like the refraction into eternity of the Passion of Christ' (IC 70). Consequently the resemblances between the two stories 'can only confirm, and not weaken, the Christian dogma' (IC 71).

While Greek literature and philosophy were her first loves, Weil also drew comparisons between Christian tradition and other religious traditions. Of the living religions, she familiarized herself with Buddhist and Hindu Scriptures in particular, and drew conclusions about the presence of divine truth in them similar to those within the myth of Prometheus. She also greatly admired the Egyptian cult of Osiris and the religion of the Cathars of the Languedoc. She concluded that:

> Every time that a man has, with a pure heart called upon Osiris, Dionysus, Krishna, Buddha, the Tao etc., the Son of God has answered him by sending the Holy Spirit. (GWG 114)

Common to all of these religions (although not, in Weil's opinion, common to other religions such as Islam or Judaism) was a crucial insight which 'proved' the divine truth was present within them. This insight was the holy beauty of suffering. Infinitely more than resurrection, it was suffering which was the mark of divine presence in a religion. 'Hitler,' she argued,

> could die and return to life again fifty times, but I should still not look upon him as the Son of God. And if the Gospel omitted all mention of Christ's resurrection, faith would be easier for me. The Cross by itself suffices me. For me the proof, the really miraculous thing, is the perfect beauty of the accounts of the Passion. (GWG 129)

The implications of Weil's beliefs for inter-faith dialogue are not hard to see. It is also not difficult to understand why some Christians with whom she shared her views judged them heretical. Her discernment of divine truth in other religions might well be thought to compromise the traditional affirmation of the uniqueness of Christ. As problematic as any other aspect of Weil's theology, however, is her fierce repudiation of the Old Testament and Jewish faith. It will be recalled that Weil had rejected her Jewish ancestry in an excessively forthright way. That she did so while so many Jews were being murdered by the Nazis makes it all the more urgent that her attitude towards the Jews is challenged.

Weil argued that Moses, the greatest prophet of the Jews, knew about the divine truth present in other religions, but chose wilfully to reject it. The Hebrews, she suggested, far from understanding affliction as a gateway to God's truth, believed it to be a symptom of the sinfulness of the sufferer. Suffering was God's punishment of sinful people. With the exception of the Book of Job, and a few passages in Isaiah, all of Jewish Scripture was concerned solely with the worship of power. She had, she continued,

always been kept away from Christianity by its ranking these stories, so full of pitiless cruelty, as sacred texts ... I have never been able to understand how it is possible for a reasonable mind to regard the Jehovah of the Bible and the Father who is invoked in the Gospel as one and the same being. (SL 129–30)

She took this rejection of the Jewish origins of Christianity to often bizarre extremes. Ignoring the overwhelming historical evidence to the contrary, Weil argued that far from being thoroughly Jewish: 'The Gospels are the last and most marvellous expression of Greek genius' (IC 52).

She even speculated that the Lord's Prayer had originally been spoken in Greek, because of the beauty of the prayer in the Greek New Testament. The 'madness' of this aspect of her thought is to some observers frankly repugnant, and her mistrust of the Jews uncharacteristically loveless. It also raises serious questions about her understanding of Christianity and of truth which will be taken up again briefly in Chapter 5.

God's Existence

In simple terms, responses to the question of God's existence fall into three categories: theism (belief in God), atheism (rejection of belief in God), and agnosticism (belief that the existence or non-existence of God cannot be known with certainty). To Weil, however, these categories misrepresent the complexity of God's existence. It is not possible to speak of God's existence, she argued, without eventually coming up against contradictions. Weil was not at all worried by this, indeed she believed that contradictions can sometimes be immensely fruitful. When the imagination is confronted by apparently conflicting ideas, patient reflection upon them occasionally yields powerful insights into truth. An obvious example is the doctrine of the Trinity: God is one, and God is three persons. Another example is the mystery of the cross, which is both a freewill offering and a punishment.

For Weil, God's existence can also be expressed as a contradiction:

> *A case of contradictories which are true: God exists: God does not exist. Where is the problem? I am quite sure that there is a God in the sense that I am quite sure my love is not illusory. I am quite sure that there is not a God in the sense that I am quite sure nothing real can be like what I am able to conceive when I pronounce this word. But that which I cannot conceive is not an illusion.* (GG 103)

What does Weil mean by saying that nothing real can correspond to what we imagine when we say the word 'God'? Weil recognized that human needs are incredibly powerful. So powerful is our need to be loved, for example, that we distort the reality of the beloved so that they match our needs. The person we love may not love us, but we want them to so much that we imagine our feelings are reciprocated. Instead of loving someone for who they are, we love them as who we would like them to be. This represents a flaw in the human imagination which can also occur when we try and imagine God. When we imagine God, how can we know that we are not conjuring up a false picture simply because of the force of our need for a particular kind of god? Weil's answer is that we cannot know. The only solution is to let go of imagining God's existence altogether, and to let God be God. For this reason, Weil can say that:

> *Of two men who have no experience of God, he who denies him is perhaps nearer to him than the other. The false God who is like the true one in everything, except that we cannot touch him, prevents us from ever coming to the true one. We have to believe in a God who is like the true God in everything, except that he does not exist, since we have not yet reached the point where God exists.* (GG 103)

Weil's argument might lead us in several directions. One direction might be to become so frustrated with the impossibility of faith that we give up and become agnostic. But Weil does not draw this conclusion from her own arguments. Far from excluding contemplation of God's truth, awareness of the contradiction of God's existence opens up the possibility of genuine attention to God. If Weil is right, for example, that it is impossible to speak about God without making God into what we want him to be in our imaginations, then the limitations of dogma as the basis of faith begin to become clear. Jesus said: 'Not everyone who says to me "Lord, Lord," will enter the kingdom of heaven, but only the one who does the will of my Father in heaven' (Matthew 7:21). Weil argued that there is no value in thinking that just because we believe in a particular doctrine, for example that Jesus is Lord, we have achieved anything. Weil concluded that:

The dogmas of the faith are not things to be affirmed. They are things to be regarded from a certain distance, with attention, respect and love. They are like the bronze serpent [cf. Numbers 21:8–9] whose virtue is such that whoever looks upon it shall live. This attentive and loving gaze, by a shock on the rebound, causes a source of light to flash on the soul which illuminates all aspects of human life on this earth. Dogmas lose this virtue as soon as they are affirmed. (GWG 125–6)

Thus, the only legitimate response to religious mysteries in the Christian tradition or in any other, is not to affirm doctrines, but to love God. The truly important religious question is not 'Are you saved?' or 'Do you believe in God?' but 'Do you love God with the whole of your attention?'.

One feature of Weil's proposals about loving God remains particularly difficult to grasp. Weil had argued that we must let go of God's existence, since it is impossible to hold God in our imaginations without distorting him. But if God cannot be imagined, if dogmas about God are intrinsically flawed, how do we know what God is like in order to love him? How do we know that God is like a loving Father and not merely some malicious super-being? Weil argued, as we have seen, that we are to 'believe in a God who is like the true God in everything, except that he does not exist'. However, for Weil, this does not mean that we cannot say anything about God. Compare one hundred real pound coins, and one hundred imaginary pound coins. There are some differences between them; one can spend the real coins but not the imaginary ones, for instance. However, we can say some things about the imaginary coins and still make perfect sense. Even though they are imaginary, there are still exactly one hundred coins, not one pound more, not one less. In an analogous way, Weil believed that we can still say of the 'imaginary' God that he is loving, good, just, and so on. She noted:

Nothing which exists is absolutely worthy of love. We must therefore love that which does not exist. This non-existent object of love is not a fiction, however, for our fictions cannot be any more worthy of love than we ourselves, and we are not worthy of it. (GG 99–100)

Thus, even though Weil insisted that we must believe in God as though he does not exist, we can still *genuinely* love him. It is thus in the light of Weil's rejection of dogma, and her redefinition of faith as attentive love towards God, that proper meaning can be made of the affirmation that Weil made in her last months to a friend:

I believe in God, in the Trinity, in the Incarnation, in the Redemption, in the teachings of the Gospel.

Waiting on God

Weil established that the proper aim of someone seeking God is not belief, but attention. What Weil meant by attention, however, is not immediately obvious. The French word Weil uses (*attente*) conveys the sense both of attention and of waiting. What Weil attempted to communicate with the concept is both an attitude of readiness to God, and a kind of patient non-activity. The purest form of this attention, for Weil, is prayer; indeed:

Attention, taken to its highest degree, is the same thing as prayer. It presupposes faith and love. Absolutely unmixed action is prayer. (GG 105–6)

Such attentiveness to God has widespread ramifications for daily life:

[It] makes certain things impossible for us. Such is the non-acting action of prayer in the soul. There are ways of behaviour which would

veil such attention should they be indulged in and which, reciprocally, this attention puts out of the question. (GG 107-8)

One such pattern of behaviour precluded by a life of attention to God is excessive attachment to this world. While 'non-attachment' to the world is a prominent feature of many religious traditions, Weil believed that in the Christian tradition this kind of prayerful life had been kept alive only by mystics, such as St John of the Cross (1540-1591). Weil believed strongly that 'detachment' should be an essential component of all Christian faith. Detachment is 'non-active' in that it does not seek the fulfilment of any personal need, but involves emptying oneself of all desire. Detachment means, for Weil,

to empty desire, finality of all content, to desire in the void, to desire without any wishes. To detach our desire from all good things and to wait. Experience proves that this waiting is satisfied. It is then that we touch the absolute good. (GG 13)

As with her theology of the existence and non-existence of God, there is a contradiction present in the notion of detachment from desire as the way to achieve fulfilment:

We can only possess what we renounce; what we do not renounce escapes from us. In this sense, we cannot possess anything whatever unless it passes through God. (GG 29)

Weil thought that a fundamental dilemma of human existence is that on the one hand we are driven by our needs, but on the other hand, our needs are never actually satisfied. On the simplest level, for instance, we are hungry so we eat, but our satisfaction is only ever temporary, and soon we become hungry again. Even in more important matters, it is human nature never to be completely satisfied. A person may want a particular job, get it, and soon after want another, better job. This merry-go-round of desire gets in the way of attentiveness to God. Even on a more mundane level it means that most people expend themselves seeking for something that can never actually be achieved. This is an invidious situation and results in most people being very unhappy part of the time, and partly unhappy all of the time. It is to this end that the art of detachment is so crucial in achieving a genuine attentiveness to God. Just as in relation to the existence of God the believer must adopt the strategy of emptying the imagination of the existence of God, so with prayerful attention, they must adopt the strategy of emptying themselves of desire.

Weil's theology of detachment may appear at first to be a technique or method, through which a person may attain God by exercising acquired skills in prayerful attentiveness. 'Weil suggests,' this interpretation might say, 'that if you follow these steps you will achieve perfect happiness'. However, Weil did *not* intend her theology of detachment to be a step by step guide to the knowledge of God and the attainment of personal happiness. Part of what is meant by giving up one's desires, she believed, is giving up even the desire for personal salvation. Weil also maintained that because God is separated from us by an infinity of space and time, there is nothing that human beings can do to take even one step towards God:

> *We cannot take a single step towards the heavens. God crosses the universe and comes to us.*
> *Over the infinity of time and space, the infinitely more infinite love of God comes to possess us. He comes at his own time. We have the power to consent to receive him or to refuse.* (WG 73-4)

Weil makes it crystal clear that our waiting on God cannot bring God one step closer, for the coming of God is a *gift*. What the believer offers by her attentiveness is simply her consent to God's presence.

The principle of non-attachment to personal desire and to the world was, Weil believed, an essential characteristic of faith in many traditions though particularly of Buddhism (it is no coincidence that at the same time Weil was developing these thoughts in Marseilles, she was also studying Buddhist Scriptures). Weil, however, developed the concept further and went on to speak of *decreation* of the self in attentiveness to God. The initiative for this, Weil believed, came from God himself, who renounced his power in creation, and even his existence, to die on a cross. Just as God is emptied of divinity in the abandonment of Christ on the cross, so should the believer, Weil continued, renounce themselves in order to respond to God. In the eucharist, she adds, God goes so far as to be *consumed* by the believer, and invites the believer to reciprocate by offering their being to be consumed by God.

God gave me being in order that I should give it back to him.(GG 35)

Except the seed die [cf. John 12:24] ... it has to die in order to liberate the energy it bears within it so that with this energy new forms may be developed. So we have to die in order to liberate a tied up *energy, in order to possess an energy which is free and capable of understanding the true relationship of things.* (GG 30)

Does decreation mean then that a believer's aim is to *eliminate* her own unique self, to wipe out her individuality as far as humanly possible? This important question is not easy to answer. It is certainly true that there are passages in Weil's notebooks in which she writes of the self, or the 'I' as she sometimes calls it, as something to be overridden.

The sin in me says 'I' ... It is because of my wretchedness that I am 'I'. (GG 27)

The self is only the shadow which sin and error cast by stopping the light of God, and I take this shadow for a being. (GG 35)

However, this was not, for Weil, the same thing as believing that the self is something *bad*. For her, the natural desires of the self get in the way of God. Weil was careful to distinguish decreation of the self, and destruction of the self. To destroy something meant to make it cease to exist, to become nothing. Decreating the self, however, meant transforming it from something that belonged to the natural world, into something that belonged to God. Decreation was a continuation of the phrase in the Lord's prayer which asks that 'Thy will be done'. She hoped that by means of decreation, her own needs would cease to get in the way of God's love for the world:

If only I knew how to disappear there would be a perfect union of love between God and the earth I tread, the sea I hear ... May I disappear in order that those things that I see may become perfect in their beauty from the very fact that they are no longer things that I see. (GG 36-7)

As I suggested in Chapter 1, mystical theology is by its nature difficult to comprehend. Weil's understanding of attention and waiting on God, and their practice through detachment and decreation of the self, are not best read as abstract intellectual proposals – they belong in the realm of the spirit. These spiritual reflections are not intended as subjects for discussion, but for practice. Weil once observed:

Human thought and the universe constitute the books of revelation par excellence, if the attention, lighted by love and faith, knows how to decipher them. The reading of them is a proof, and indeed the only certain proof. After having read the Iliad *in Greek, no one would dream of wondering whether the professor who taught him the Greek alphabet had deceived him.* (IC 201)

The only way to 'prove' the value of Weil's 'grammar' of the spiritual life is to become attentive to God, to detach oneself from the world, and to decreate one's own ego.

3

Loving God in a World Full of Pain

For anyone who experiences suffering or who thinks about the suffering of others, one profound question becomes insistent: Why must people suffer? For those who believe in God, the question is even more urgent. If God is powerful and loving, why does he allow people to suffer? Is it because he is not all-powerful? Is it because he is not, after all, a loving God, and allows suffering or, worse still, causes it to happen out of malice? As Weil observed, the question 'Why?' is so inevitable as a reaction to suffering that on the cross even Christ himself asked it: 'My God, my God, why have you forsaken me?' If we are to love God then it is vital that we find a way of coming to terms with this question.

The Law of Gravity

Weil identified a major obstacle which gets in the way of a proper understanding of suffering. She considered that the perception most people have of the world is so corrupt, base and superficial that, confronted with suffering, they cannot see beyond their own experience to the wider view necessary to resolve the question. The first step towards coming to terms with suffering, Weil believed, is to understand something about the forces that press upon the human soul, and about the nature and reality of this world. In order to describe the condition of human life, and the reality of the world Weil used two concepts which are extremely difficult to understand: *gravity* and *necessity*. Before examining the first of these, it is useful to recall Weil's life-long fascination with mathematics and science.

It is said that above the door of the Academy the philosopher Plato established in Athens he had written the words: 'Let no one ignorant of mathematics enter here'. This was a sentiment that Weil entirely agreed with. For her, the insights afforded by philosophy and theology were inextricably interwoven with the insights of mathematics and science. Her notebooks are peppered with algebraic formulae, and with mathematical diagrams which illustrate her thought. It seemed perfectly sensible for Weil to translate what she knew about geometry, physics, or biological science into her own philosophical writings. One way she did this was by means of *analogy*, that is, by observing the agreement or similarity between certain specific characteristics of the laws of science and the 'laws' of the human soul and the realities of human life. In one sense, Weil's analogies involve nothing more than drawing illustrations from the world of science and employing them like a poet might employ a metaphor – to bring colour and clarity to her philosophical argument. However, occasionally she uses an analogy so frequently and consistently that it seems as though she intended more than a poetic comparison. Her use of the terms gravity and necessity fall into this second pattern.

One of the most important of the analogies Weil used was her comparison of the laws of gravity and the laws which govern the inner life of the human soul:

> All the natural *movements of the soul are controlled by laws analogous to those of physical gravity.* (GG 1)

Each person who has not turned towards God, she argued, far from being a free agent – able to choose who they are and what they do – is subject to laws of the soul, just as a falling stone is subject to the laws of physical gravity. (In French, Weil uses the word *pesanteur* for gravity, which can also mean 'heaviness' or 'sluggishness'.) 'The law of gravity,' she maintained, 'which is sovereign on earth over all material motion is the image of the carnal attachment which governs the tendencies of the soul' (SNLG 151). Unless God intervenes, this moral law of gravity determines the behaviour of the soul and makes it behave in predictable ways. Gravity, for example, is the reason why, when someone needs us, one of our natural reactions is to pull away; our soul reacts as if pushed by an unseen force as powerful as the force of gravity. When her headaches were particularly violent, Weil noted, she longed intensely for others to experience the same suffering as herself. This too, she believed, was evidence of the force of gravity on her soul. It is gravity that forces the soul to conform to society's values and needs instead of paying attention to God.

The natural impulse of the soul to behave in such ways was, for Weil, similar to what theologians might describe as a tendency of human beings to sin. Although she never wrote that human subjection to moral gravity was identical to behaving immorally, Weil made it clear that to be unthinkingly obedient to the impulses of human nature is to commit a great sin.

However, just as gravity was not the only physical law governing physical life on the planet, moral gravity was, to Weil, not the only law governing the life of the human soul. In addition to the law of gravity which causes the soul to sink into corruption, there is another force which leads it to God:

Two forces rule the universe: light and gravity. (GG 1)

The only force powerful enough to overcome the effects of physical gravity is solar energy. In a frequently repeated image, Weil described how the force of *grace* operates on the soul like light on a plant. Imagine the life of a seed that germinates beneath a heavy slab of concrete. The force of gravity presses down on the concrete, which in turn presses down onto the plant. However, miraculously, the young plant is so attracted to the sun that it is able to find its way through the smallest crack in the concrete, and grow upwards into the light. Thus, the force of light is able to defeat the laws of gravity as light is transformed into the energy which enables the plant to grow. Human beings cannot help having the natural impulses Weil describes as moral gravity, but they can choose to be blindly obedient to them, or to reach towards God like a plant grows towards light.

Weil pressed this analogy even further. *All* energy on earth, she continued, comes either directly or indirectly from the sun. Plants transform the energy contained within light and store it. This energy enters into animals when plants are eaten. Alternatively, the energy is stored in wood, coal, or oil. Thus, the direct energy of the sun is buried and hidden until it is dug up and burned as fuel. Weil proposed that this summary of the nature of energy 'is the image of grace, which comes down to be buried in the darkness of our souls and is the only source of energy which can counteract the trend towards evil which is the moral law of gravity' (SNLG 151).

Grace, like energy, cannot be taken, only received. All a farmer can do, she added, is to arrange his farm in such a way that his animals and plants can receive this energy. In a similar way, no one can go out and take grace – all they can do is to so dispose their souls that they will be able to receive the gift of grace. To dispose the soul to light, however, involves first of all acknowledging that it is subject to gravity. Not everyone achieves this. Most people live in the world dominated by their shallow sensations without ever realizing that they are subject to the unseen force of moral gravity.

Necessity And Obedience

The second difficult but crucial concept Weil used was that of *necessity*. Weil characterized necessity in two apparently contradictory ways. On the one hand, necessity represented for Weil the pitiless harshness of life in the world. On the other hand, necessity was the reality of God's world, calling us to be obedient to him. Let us consider first what Weil meant by describing the relentless harshness of the world as necessity.

The world is changing all the time. However, Weil argued, there are certain things about the world which in spite of its change remain consistent. One of these is its continual presence. The reality of the world is something we can never escape except by death. 'Necessity' is the name Weil gave to this characteristic of reality, its 'continual presence'. Weil knew that one common Christian understanding of the world is that after creation, God continues to be involved in the world by means of his *providence*, that is, that God cares for and protects his creatures in their life in the world. However, for Weil, this understanding is fraught with difficulties. If we believe in God's providence, why, we must ask, does he seem sometimes to protect some of his creatures from harm, while at other times they are given up to suffering? When a child is suffering with cancer, for example, why should their healing be seen as God's providential intervention, while a child in the next hospital bed goes on to die? Weil's explanation is that God does not act providentially in the world at all. On the contrary:

The creation is an abandonment. In creating what is other than Himself, God necessarily abandoned it ... God abandons our entire being – flesh, blood, sensibility, intelligence, love – to the pitiless necessity of matter and the cruelty of the devil, except for the eternal and supernatural part of the soul. (FLN 103)

The death of one child and the survival of the other have nothing to do with God's providence, Weil believed, but both result from the necessity of creation. Creation is not, she thought, 'good' (as the Book of Genesis suggests), but neither is it bad – it is simply necessary. For Weil, therefore, the first step in coming to terms with the 'Why?' of suffering, is to understand that the question is unanswerable. Behind the joys and sufferings of our life there is not a hidden divine plan, as Christians have traditionally affirmed. Thus, 'There can be no answer to the 'Why?' of the afflicted, because the world is necessity and not purpose' (GWG 101).

To elaborate on this idea, Weil cited one of the sayings of Jesus (Matthew 5:45): 'The sun shines on the just and on the unjust ... God makes himself *necessity*' (GG 38). Just as the sun shines on men and women irrespective of their moral qualities, so too does the rain fall upon them. Good and bad happen to us not for a purpose, but because the mechanism of necessity is blind. To Weil, a crucial insight is that both sun and rain, affliction and joy, come from God. Thus, she argued, 'It is in his Providence that God has willed that necessity should be like a blind mechanism' (WG 67).

The death of one child and survival of the other, she continued, is not at all arbitrary or malicious. Such experience is simply the *necessity* of human life. One consequence of this is that while the question 'Why?' is inevitable for those who suffer, ultimately it is a question that cannot be answered:

There is a question which is absolutely meaningless and therefore, of course, unanswerable, and which we normally never ask ourselves, but in affliction the soul is constrained to speak it incessantly like a sustained monotonous groan. This question is: Why? Why are things as they are? The afflicted man naïvely seeks an answer, from men, from things, from God, even if he disbelieves in him, from anything or everything ... If one explained to him the causes which have produced his present situation, and this is in any case seldom possible because of the complex interaction of circumstances, it will not seem to him to be an answer. For his question 'Why?' does not mean 'By what cause?' but 'For what purpose?' (GWG 100)

The value of this aspect of necessity is, therefore, that it is 'an image by which the mind can conceive of the indifference, the impartiality of God' (GG 94). However, there was, for Weil, a second way of regarding necessity, and that is to love it:

One must tenderly love the harshness of that necessity which is like a coin with two faces, the one turned towards us being domination and the one turned towards God, obedience. We must embrace it closely even if it offers its roughest surface and the roughness cuts into us. Any lover is glad to clasp tightly some object belonging to an absent loved one, even to the point where it cuts into the flesh. We know that this universe is an object belonging to God. (SNLG 196)

To Weil, though no one can choose to opt out of the world that is governed by necessity, people do have a choice about how they react to it. Weil believed that just as the laws of mathematics come from God, so too does necessity. The choice facing each person is whether or not they will submit to necessity, or strain fruitlessly against it:

We have to consent to be subject to necessity and to act only by handling it ... Obedience is the supreme virtue. We have to love necessity. (GG 38)

Sometimes, obeying this mechanism of necessity fits in naturally with our own immediate needs. When we are hungry, for instance, our obedience to necessity leads us to satisfy our hunger by eating. However, sometimes obedience to necessity means transcending our natural desires. Weil illustrated this point vividly:

If my eternal salvation were on this table in the form of an object and if I only had to stretch out my hand to grasp it, I would not stretch out my hand without having received orders to do so. (GG 39)

As with the light which can lead one out from the heaviness of the moral law of gravity, so too with obedience to necessity: it cannot ever be taken, it can only ever be received as a gift. As an illustration, Weil recalled Jesus' saying about the lilies of the field (Matthew 6:28), which are more beautiful than King Solomon in all his glory, although they make no effort other than to be docile in their submission to natural necessity. To Weil, once the impartiality of God given necessity is accepted, the beauty of the world begins to shine through:

The beauty of the world appears when we recognise that the substance of the universe is necessity and that the substance of necessity is obedience to a perfectly wise Love. The universe of which we are a fraction has no other essence than to be obedient. (GWG 90)

Weil's solution to the difficulties of the traditional Christian theology of providence is highly original. Moreover, Weil rightly acknowledges that even if God can be described as 'abandoning' creation to the blind laws of necessity, he is still, as its creator, responsible for those laws. Even if we accept, therefore, that impartial necessity leads some to suffer and others to happiness, some way must still be found of loving the God who creates a world in which affliction occurs. Weil's proposal about how this is possible is one of her best-known and important contributions to religious thought.

The Love of God and Affliction

Weil's analysis of these questions used the word *malheur* – meaning not merely unhappiness or sorrow, but affliction – a condition compounded of pain and distress. Weil began by making an important distinction between *suffering* and *affliction*.

Affliction, Weil argued, 'is inseparable from physical suffering and yet quite distinct' (WG 62). It is perfectly possible, she wrote, to experience suffering without experiencing affliction. Take the example of toothache. At the time one experiences toothache, it can be excruciatingly painful. However, an hour or two after it has been fixed, it is easily forgotten; it leaves no mark on the soul. Suffering of physical pain on its own causes neither degradation nor hopelessness. Affliction, on the other hand, reaches deep down inside the soul. It is, she wrote,

... an uprooting of life, a more or less attenuated equivalent of death, made irresistibly present to the soul by the attack or immediate apprehension of physical pain. If there is complete absence of physical pain there is no affliction for the soul, because our thoughts can turn to no matter what object ... Here below physical pain, and that alone, has the power to chain down our thoughts ... (WG 62)

But, it might be objected, there are many terrible human experiences that apparently have no element of physical pain, and yet are profoundly hurtful to the soul. To Weil, this was quite true. However, her definition of 'physical pain' included several kinds of experiences in which the body is outwardly undamaged. To Weil, for example, fear of torture should be regarded as causing physical pain, even though the body remains untouched. Similarly, when a loved one dies, even though there is no bodily wound, the grief that follows is experienced as though it was a physical pain, with difficulty in breathing, a sensation of unfulfilled need, even of hunger for the person who has been lost. Furthermore, when simple physical pain extends over a long time, its repetitive recurrence can lead the soul into genuine affliction. To Weil, this insight was clear from her own debilitating migraine headaches.

For Weil then, the defining characteristic of affliction is that it is total. There is not real affliction 'unless the event which has seized and uprooted a life attacks it ... in all its parts, social, psychological and physical' (WG 63).

To a person in the grip of genuine affliction, God seems absent, the soul is filled with horror as it is flung an infinite distance from God, and time stretches on ahead filled with nothing but interminable pain. To Weil, such affliction is so horrific that the soul would rather escape from affliction than death. In the light of this description, one truth about affliction becomes crystal clear:

> It is wrong to desire affliction; it is against nature, and it is a perversion; and moreover it is the essence of affliction that it is suffered unwillingly. (GWG 87–8)

Total affliction, Weil believed, is rarer than one might imagine. To be created does not necessarily expose us to affliction, but only to its possibility. Most instances of suffering carry within them seeds of consolation. To be genuine affliction, suffering must be pure and unmitigated. Thus, for example, Weil believed that the early Christian martyrs who drew consolation in their tortures from the hope of salvation after death were not truly experiencing affliction, for their suffering was consoled by the possibility of reward. Those who suffer on behalf of a cause have their suffering mitigated because there is meaning in their suffering. In contrast, the cross of Christ, which was always Weil's model for affliction, was a criminal's death, not that of a martyr, and was characterized not by its meaning, but by the fact that Jesus was exposed to ridicule. His affliction, she was convinced, was not mitigated by the knowledge that he would rise again, it was total, and his final cry – 'It is finished' – were the final words of a dying man.

Weil's description of affliction is all-encompassing. It is all the more startling, therefore when, in a letter to Joë Bousquet, a friend who was permanently paralysed as a result of a wound received during the First World War, Weil described his afflicted state as 'privileged' and 'fortunate'. If affliction is so terrible, why on earth should anyone be regarded as privileged who is forced to experience it? Weil's answer is that the privilege of affliction lies not in any intrinsic value, but in the fact that the truth of Christianity consists in a proper understanding of it. It would be a monstrous misrepresentation of God to assert that he causes affliction, even if he does so in order to teach humankind some eternal truth. To Weil, suffering was plainly evil, and consequently 'affliction in itself contains no gift from above' (GWG 95). Nevertheless, she maintained that 'knowledge of affliction is the key of Christianity' (GWG 91).

The first reason that affliction may be spoken of as a privilege is that when accepted obediently it is a way of encountering the reality of the world's necessity. Imagine greeting a close friend whom we have not seen for a long time. On meeting them, the friend grips our hand so tightly that it causes pain. However, Weil suggested, our reaction to this pain is to be glad of it, for the painful handshake confirms to us the reality of the friend's presence. Similarly, affliction, when it pierces the soul, signals an experience in which a true encounter is taking place with creation and the creator. It is, therefore, to be welcomed.

Affliction enables a person to participate in the affliction of the world and of people within it. In her letter to Bousquet Weil wrote:

> You are specially privileged in that the present state of the world is a reality for you ... you are infinitely privileged, because you have war permanently lodged in your body ... To think affliction, it is necessary to bear it in one's flesh, driven very far in like a nail, and for a long time, so that thought may have time to grow strong enough to regard it. (SL 136–7)

Our natural instinct is always to flee from affliction. The feeling of revulsion towards affliction is so extreme that the afflicted person will usually turn inwards upon themselves to escape from it. However, in the middle of the Second World War, Weil believed that Bousquet was privileged because the experience of the horror of war was imprinted upon his suffering body. The experience of pain, she continued, is the pain of the universe entering the body. Weil recalled how, in the factory, when an apprentice suffered a minor injury, the more experienced workers would comment that the wound was the trade entering the apprentice's body. Most people are taken completely unawares by their affliction, they are crushed by it and have no opportunity to come to terms with it, or to allow it to become a part of their understanding of the world. Bousquet, however had the 'opportunity and the function of knowing the truth of the world's affliction and contemplating its reality' (SL 137). It is only by learning to understand affliction in this way that one can have a proper understanding of the affliction of others.

A second reason why affliction is the key to Christianity is that as well as being necessary in order to enter into the suffering of others, it is also the way by which we may enter into the suffering of God:

Affliction is truly at the centre of Christianity ... What we are commanded to love first of all is affliction: the affliction of man, the affliction of God. (GWG 96)

Weil believed that in God's willingness to submit to affliction in Jesus lay the most important truth about his love for the world. Returning to the classic problem of evil, she wrote:

Either God is not almighty or he is not absolutely good, or else he does not command everywhere where he has the power to do so.
Thus the existence of evil here below, far from disproving the reality of God is the very thing which reveals him in his truth. (WG 82)

The truth about God is that he not only invites human beings to submit to necessity, in his great love he also gives himself completely to it. Jesus' crucifixion is an act of supreme obedience. On the cross, God suspends his power by an act of voluntary restraint, renouncing himself. Weil's conclusion is that there is suffering in the world not because God lacks the power to change it, or the goodness to desire that it be changed. The universe was never intended by God to be a place where he could exercise his powers, rather, God deliberately restrains himself from acting there. It is only by experiencing personal affliction that this truth about God becomes clear to us, and only then do we reach towards a proper understanding of the nature of God's love. It is in affliction that we learn to *decreate* (see Chapter 2) our own perspective, and learn how to see things from God's point of view. Such insight is ultimately a gift from God.

In one of the most important and memorable comments in her notebooks Weil summarized what she was trying to say with her theology of affliction: 'The extreme greatness of Christianity lies in the fact that it does not seek a supernatural remedy for suffering but a supernatural use for it' (GG 73). Knowledge of Christianity involved, for Weil, not deliverance from suffering, but the realization that in pure affliction lies our true meeting point with the immensity of God's love.

It is important to note that although Weil saw affliction as the key to Christianity, she in no way diminished the horror of affliction or, indeed, of evil. Weil understood that one response to affliction is total disillusionment with the world. Faced with the presence of affliction in the world one might say that there is not only no God, because no God could allow affliction; but also, that there is nothing of ultimate value in the world since everything seems to be so fragile. However, Weil contended that if nothing in the world was of any value, then evil could not exist, since it would have nothing to take from us. Since we feel affliction to be evil then, plainly, there are things of value in the world. For this reason, the greater the joy we have known, the greater will be the experience of affliction when it is lost. Thus, between evil, suffering and sin, Weil perceived a complex interrelationship:

> *Evil is neither suffering nor sin; it is both at the same time, it is something common to them both. For they are linked together; sin makes us suffer and suffering makes us evil, and this indissoluble complex of suffering and sin is the evil in which we are submerged against our will and to our horror.* (GWG 76)

Although affliction must under no circumstance be sought out, not even in order to experience God, nevertheless, it is necessary to be as prepared to experience pure affliction as it is to be prepared for pure joy. Weil wrote to Bousquet:

> *I am convinced that affliction on the one hand, and on the other hand joy, when it is a complete and pure commitment to perfect beauty, are the only two keys which give entry to the realm of purity, where one can breathe: the home of the real.* (SL 141)

What unites these two keys to knowledge of God is that 'each of them must be unmixed: the joy without a shadow of incompleteness, the affliction completely unconsoled' (SL 141).

Though Weil is plain enough about the common qualities of joy and affliction, it is fair to observe that her overwhelming emphasis is on affliction. Partly, this results from what she justly perceived to be the extensive misunderstanding of affliction in Christian theology. Nevertheless, the impression left by Weil is sometimes one of imbalance. Weil's theological reserve towards the Resurrection ('The Cross by itself suffices me' (GWG 129)) is a symptom of the underdevelopment of her theology of joy compared with her theology of affliction. This is brought home in one of Weil's notebooks in which she wrote an extraordinary prayer expressing to God her complete acceptance of the possibility of affliction for herself:

Father, in the name of Christ grant me this. That I may be unable to will any bodily movement, or any attempt at movement, like a total paralytic. That I may be incapable of receiving any sensation, like someone who is completely blind, deaf and deprived of all the senses. That I may be unable to make the slightest connection between two thoughts, even the simplest ... And let me be a paralytic – blind, deaf, witless and utterly decrepit. (FLN 243–4)

The absence of a parallel prayer expressing her preparedness for total joy is a lamentable omission.

Forms of the Implicit Love of God

In affliction, Weil believed, lay the key to understanding the graciousness of God's love. God submitted himself to affliction in an act of such tremendous love that it invites a response of love from human beings. However, Weil argued that direct love of God was impossible, for 'God is not present to the soul and never yet has been so' (WG 76). But though *direct* love of God is impossible, *indirect* love of God is possible by loving certain provisional, natural realities. This indirect love Weil called the implicit love of God. Weil suggested that there are three ways in which God can be loved implicitly:

The implicit love of God can only have three immediate objects, the only three things here below in which God is really though secretly present. These are religious ceremonies, the beauty of the world and our neighbour. (WG 77)

In addition, Weil believed friendship was a form of implicit love of God that could be distinguished from that of love for our neighbour. Such forms of the implicit love for God, though veiled, are far from being poor second-bests. For the majority of people, direct love of God is never possible, and the implicit forms of love are the only way for them to love until their death. Even though for most people these forms of love never become direct, nevertheless, these implicit loves can be love *for God*, and are not under any circumstances valueless. For a few people – those who learn the lessons of affliction or joy – the implicit forms of love can grow so strong that they are subsumed and perfected, until they become direct forms of love for God. Even in its unperfected forms, implicit love of God can sometimes, Weil continued, reach a high degree of purity and power and even possess the virtue of sacraments. In any case, however, implicit forms of love for God must always precede direct love for God.

The first implicit love of God is love of our neighbour. In Matthew's gospel (Matthew 25:40), Jesus suggested that whoever gives to someone who is afflicted is in some sense giving to Christ himself. Within this statement, however, Weil perceived a paradox:

Who but Christ himself can be Christ's benefactor? How can a man give meat to Christ, if he is not raised at least for a moment to the state spoken of by Saint Paul, when he no longer lives in himself but Christ lives in him? (WG 77)

As well as being present in the person who receives as Jesus' parable suggests, Weil implied that Christ must also in some sense be present in the person who gives. What she meant by this difficult interpretation of Jesus' parable is that the spiritual worthiness of the person who gives has little to do with the value of the gift. In a service of holy communion, bread is passed from the priest to the believing communicant. But this sanctified bread is not simply being given by the priest: it is also mysteriously the gift of God. The worthiness of the priest is irrelevant, because the important thing is that it is God who gives the gift. Similarly, with an act of charity, Christ can make holy the gift of even a sinful person to someone in need. Thus, in addition to being an act of fellowship between donor and recipient, an act of charity also involves participating in the pure love of God.

Weil also believed that it is impossible to conceive of love in isolation from justice. That is to say, as well as having the qualities associated with love, an act of charity must also have within it the qualities associated with justice. When one person or group of people is in a position of power, Weil argued, their natural response is to use their position of strength to exploit the weaker party. If it is possible to do so, the strong often impose their will upon the weak. However, when confronted by a neighbour in need, Weil argued that in order to be an act of true charity, this natural relationship of inequality must somehow be overcome. Otherwise, even when giving to a needy neighbour, the stronger party will actually benefit more than the one who receives their gift. It is easy on a small scale to understand what Weil means when we think of the way that giving money to charity often makes us feel good about ourselves. It may seem as though we are giving something away, but in fact we are in some degree bolstering our need to feel generous. Weil put it most sharply when she wrote that 'Almsgiving when it is not supernatural is like a sort of purchase. It buys the sufferer' (WG 84). The result of this, she continued, is that 'Beyond a certain degree of inequality in the relations of men of unequal strength, the weaker passes into the state of matter and loses his personality' (WG 80). However, in contrast, justice means that there is between stronger and weaker parties a relationship of mutual consent: 'The supernatural virtue of justice consists of behaving exactly as though there were equality when one is the stronger in an unequal relationship' (WG 81).

Once love for our neighbour is seen in this light, it becomes clear that helping the afflicted person should be a completely instinctive act. Some Christians, Mother Teresa of Calcutta, for example, believe that when they help a person in need they do so for the Lord's sake. Weil, however, argued that a person who exercises implicit love of God in love for the neighbour: 'would not think of saying that he takes care of the afflicted for the Lord's sake; it would seem as absurd to him as it would be to say that he eats for the Lord's sake' (GWG 94).

An act of charity is not at all a conscious act of service to God, but a simple and natural response to a person in need. That it is natural, however, is to take nothing away from the value of a true act of charity. When we give to our neighbour, Weil believed a miraculous event takes place. The person giving projects him or herself into the affliction of the other person. Imagine a mother whose child is in pain. Every pain the child feels is also in a real sense felt by his or her mother. The extent of the mother's love is so great that she projects herself into her child and actually experiences their affliction with them. Weil argued that one of the consequences of true affliction is that it reduces a person from being a human being to being a thing, an object. When a master commanded a slave, the slave was not treated as a person at all, but as an object to be used. Affliction, too, reduces a person to being an object, robbing them of their human dignity. To Weil, therefore, one of the miraculous consequences of love towards the afflicted is that it restores their humanity to them. By projecting oneself into a person who has become a mere object, one gives to them the gift of one's own humanity.

This exchange of generosity and gratitude, when it is conducted in a relationship of just equality, is immensely costly to the person who gives. By sharing in the affliction of another, by becoming personally afflicted, one's own humanity is diminished; in Jesus' words one denies oneself. Weil also believed that love for one's neighbour, like other implicit loves of God, is not confined to Christians alone, but is felt and expressed by those who are not members of the Church. In Jesus' parable of the sheep and the goats (Matthew 25:31–46), those who expressed implicit love of God by caring for those in need had apparently done so without being conscious that they were loving Christ: 'When was it that we saw you hungry and gave you food ...?'

The second form of implicit love is love of the order of the world. This complements love towards our neighbour and, in common with it, requires an act of self-renunciation. One example of this love is the celebration of beauty. However, Weil argued that love for beauty was sadly absent from the Christian tradition, though she acknowledged several exceptions to this rule, amongst them the poem of Saint Francis of Assisi celebrating the beauty of creation. Beauty, Weil believed, 'is necessity which, while remaining in conformity with its own law and with that alone, is obedient to the good' (GG 135). What she meant by this is that a beautiful thing has no objective except to be beautiful. In this quality it is unique; only beauty is not the means to something else. Such true beauty is not affected by the passage of time. Thus, our appreciation of beauty on earth is one of the few ways we can encounter here below something of the nature of eternity. However, according to Weil, even the finest works of art or science cannot compare with the natural beauty of the universe created by God:

The only true beauty, the only beauty which is the real presence of God, is the beauty of the universe. Nothing which is less than the universe is beautiful. (WG 105)

The third form of implicit love of God is the love of religious practices, by which Weil meant the love that people have for a particular religious tradition. Religion, however, Weil believed is no more valuable a form of implicit love of God than the two previous forms:

God is present in religious practices, when they are pure, just as he is present in our neighbour and in the beauty of the world; in the same way and not any more. (WG 110)

Usually, the form of religion that we love depends on where we were born. A person born into a Hindu family will love God implicitly in Hindu religious practices, while a person born into a Roman Catholic family will love God in the religious practices of Catholicism. Though there are countless ways in which different religions worship God, Weil argued that the basic virtue within each of them remains the same: it lies in the recitation of the name of the Lord. Such worship nevertheless remains an implicit, not a direct form of love for God.

The beauty of religions, Weil believed, lies in the intention behind them, and not in their outward forms. Thus, the building in which worship takes place can be ugly, or the priest corrupt, or the singing out of tune – none of this matters. To illustrate what she meant, Weil suggested that when a mathematician illustrates a mathematical proof on a blackboard or a piece of paper, the straight lines she draws are often not exactly straight, nor the circles she draws exact circles. Nevertheless, the theory she is illustrating remains perfectly true in spite of her imperfect drawing. Similarly with religion, it is the purity of their content, not of their outward form which is important. The believer fixes their attention upon this purity, and it is in this looking that salvation is to be found.

To these three forms of implicit love of God, love of neighbour, love of the order of the world, and love of religious practices, Weil added pure friendship. Friendship differs from love for our neighbour in that it is directed towards a particular person known to us. Charity does not discriminate between people, but goes out both to those we know, and towards those we do not know. In friendship, on the other hand, we learn to love someone close to us. The key to this as an implicit form of the love of God is that friendship does not seek to conform the friend to our own needs. When the motive for loving a friend is that they fulfil our own needs, Weil argued, the conditions of friendship are not genuinely fulfilled. True friendship involves 'a supernatural harmony, a union of opposites' (WG 126).

Achieving this can only happen when a kind of miracle of selflessness takes place:

> *When a human being is attached to another by a bond of affection*
> *which contains any degree of necessity, it is impossible that he should*
> *wish autonomy to be preserved both in himself and in the other. It is*
> *impossible by virtue of the mechanism of nature. It is however made*
> *possible by the miraculous intervention of the supernatural. This mir-*
> *acle is friendship.* (WG 127)

Each of these implicit forms of love for God, according to Weil, take place only where Christ is present, even when they take place outside the boundaries of the institutional Church amongst non-Christians. Where they do happen, a path is opened up for the coming of God. Weil concluded that the indirect or implicit loves of God are somehow perfected when direct love between an individual and God occurs. Far from becoming worthless after direct love has taken place, implicit forms of the love of God become a part of our direct love for God.

> *Our neighbour, our friends, religious ceremonies, and the beauty of*
> *the world do not fall to the level of unrealities after the soul has had*
> *direct contact with God. On the contrary, it is only then that these*
> *things become real. Previously they were half dreams. Previously*
> *there was no reality.* (WG 135)

One obvious question raised by Weil's exploration of implicit love for God is 'What would this look like in practice?' The concrete shape of a society which expresses love for neighbour, love for the order of the world and love for religious practices led Weil into an exploration of human nature and the need for roots.

The Need for Roots

It is becoming increasingly hard to cast one's mind back to the days in which Europe was divided by an Iron Curtain separating the communist Eastern Bloc countries and the capitalist Western allies. The collapse of the Berlin Wall in 1989 rewrote the political map of Europe. If Europe's political map has changed radically, so also has its economy. During Simone Weil's lifetime the economy of Europe was dominated by heavy industry which today has been decimated by technological, social and political change. The numbers of those employed in factories have fallen, and the nature of the work for those who remain would be barely recognizable to Weil. In places where factories once stood, there are now new employers: shopping centres filled with imported goods or leisure complexes with bowling alleys and multi-screen cinemas. Because Europe has changed, many of the political and economic theories that were current in the 1930s and 1940s have become outdated. It is to Weil's immense credit that although they originate in a very different world, her insights concerning work and society are as relevant today as they were when she first developed them.

Oppression and Liberty

Wherever there was a choice to be made, Weil was on the side of the underdog. The writings of Karl Marx (1818–1883) were an obvious initial resource for someone seeking to understand how the poor are oppressed. Weil believed that Marx had given 'a first-rate account of the mechanism of capitalist oppression' (OL 40). As Weil noted, Marx's great discovery was that social oppression was not arbitrary or accidental, but happened as a direct result of the way in which modern societies worked:

For Marx showed clearly that the true reason for the exploitation of the workers is not any desire on the part of the capitalists to enjoy and consume, but the need to expand the undertaking as rapidly as possible so as to make it more powerful than its rivals. (OL 40)

Marx believed, rightly according to Weil, that ideas should lead to action and that philosophy should aim to change the world. But to change things, one must first understand how different groups in society depend on or exploit one another. It should not be assumed that the workings of society and the economy are wholly random. Rather,

A methodological improvement in social organization presupposes a detailed study of the method of production, in order to try to find out on the one hand what we may expect from it, in the immediate or distant future, from the point of view of output, and on the other hand what forms of social and cultural organization are compatible with it, and finally, how it may itself be transformed. (OL 45-6)

Such methodical study is now called the materialistic method, but there was a problem, Weil believed, with Marx's application of it:

The materialistic method – that method which Marx bequeathed us – is an untried instrument; no Marxist has ever really used it, beginning with Marx himself. The only really valuable idea to be found in Marx's writings is also the only one that has been completely neglected. (OL 46)

Instead, what Marx had unwittingly achieved was to build a series of myths into a system without any real content.

One barrier to understanding Marx's thought and achievement was that Marxists took this flawed system and transformed it into an unchangeable doctrine. Weil, however, insisted that not even Marx was more precious than truth:

> *To my mind, it is not events which make a revision of Marxism a necessity, it is Marx's doctrine, which, because of the gaps and inconsistencies it contains, is and always has been far inferior to the role people have wanted to make it play; which does not mean to say that either then or since anything better has been worked out.* (OL 147)

The 'Red Virgin' also had something to say about another myth of the left – revolution. 'The word "revolution",' she wrote, 'is a word for which you kill, for which you die, for which you send the labouring masses to their death, but which does not possess any content' (OL 55). Why, Weil questioned, should society get better because of a revolution? Marx assumed, without concrete evidence, that societies progress through several recognizable stages, from rural to industrial, and through revolution to an idealized communist system. But, Weil insisted, 'The future is made of the same stuff as the present' (SNLG 148).

From her knowledge of Soviet Russia, Weil could see that even if the working class did stage a revolution, their situation is not greatly altered. Even with different rulers, the Russian working class continued to labour in the factories without proper reward. It did not matter who owned the means of production if factory life continued to be oppressive. As long as workers felt like cogs in the factory machine, it did not matter whether it was a capitalist 'baron' who employed them, or the Soviet state.

Weil became increasingly sure that the answer to oppression of working people must lie beyond Marxist doctrine. By 1933 she concluded:

*I have decided to withdraw entirely from any kind of political activity
except for theoretical work. That does not absolutely exclude possible
participation in a great spontaneous movement of the masses (in the
ranks, as a soldier), but I don't want any responsibility ... because I
am certain that all the blood that will be shed will be shed in vain.*

(QUOTED DAVID MCLELLAN, *SIMONE WEIL: UTOPIAN PESSIMIST,* 66)

The Experience of Work

One of the most important reasons, Weil thought, why left-wing
thinkers had not understood the limitations of their theory was
that none of them had experienced physical labour. When, in
1934, Weil began work as a labourer, she anticipated being able to
reflect on her experiences in order to sharpen up her theories. It
immediately became apparent, however, that the physical and
psychological effort required to operate the factory machinery
was so intense that it would leave her neither time nor energy to
think properly:

*... the women ... are restricted to purely mechanical labour, in which
nothing is required from them except speed. And when I say mechanical labour, don't imagine that it allows of day-dreaming, much less
reflection or thought.* (SL 11)

Weil also found herself unable to keep up with the required rates of
work:

*Yesterday I was on the same job the whole day (stamping press). I
worked until 4 o'clock at the rate of 400 pieces an hour ... and I felt
I was working hard. At 4 o'clock the foreman came round and said
that if I didn't do 800 he would get rid of me.* (SL 17)

She attributed her inability to keep up to her unfamiliarity with
physical work, her bodily awkwardness, her headaches, and her

habit of thinking too much. She concluded that to cope with factory life one must either be detached or 'fall to the vegetative level'. So unsuited was she to the work that she believed 'they would throw me out if I wasn't protected by influence' (SL 11). Worse than the physical hardship however, was the overall effect of factory life on Weil and on those around her. Socialist and communist art had idealized the workers in picture and sculpture striding powerfully into a post-capitalist future. In contrast, what Weil saw around her in the factory were men and women being stripped bare of their human dignity. Several ingredients contributed to this process of dehumanization. One ingredient was the way the foremen habitually humiliated the workers in their charge. Weil recorded one such incident in her journal:

> *The machine's belt was adjusted before I worked on it, but incorrectly, it seems, for it rides over the edge. Mouquet [the foreman] orders it shut off ... and says to Biol, 'The pulley has shifted, that's why the belt rides off'. Biol, eyeing the belt thoughtfully, starts a sentence: 'No ...' and Mouquet interrupts him: 'What do you mean, No! I say Yes! ...' Biol, without a word of reply, goes to find the guy in charge of repairs. As for me, fierce desire to slap Mouquet for his peremptory manner and his humiliatingly authoritarian tone of voice.* (FW 170)

But it was not merely a few obnoxious individuals that made factory life degrading. Weil believed that there was something wrong at a much deeper level. Of profound significance was the 'mystery' of the machine. The manufacture of a finished product had been broken up into dozens of separate processes, each machine performing only one part in an overall process of production. To the workers, the way these different processes fitted together was a complete mystery. The effect of this was to make the human machine operators feel as though they themselves were part of the machinery. Without understanding the principles of production the workers experienced no sense of participation in the process. They had no pride in their work, and turned up each day purely and simply in order to earn enough money to feed themselves and their families. Weil viewed this way of life with horror:

... to work in order to eat, to eat in order to work ... A squirrel turning in its cage ... The great hardship in manual work is that we are compelled to expend our efforts for such long hours simply in order to exist. The slave is he to whom no good is proposed as the object of his labour except mere existence. (GG 158-9)

It was degrading, she believed, to labour without any other goal than survival.

After her year in the factory was over, Weil began to tease out her tangled thoughts about work. Several practical improvements to factory life were immediately apparent to her. In order to counterbalance the effects of the mass-production line, Weil had two suggestions. First, she was convinced that labourers needed the ugliness of their lives complementing with beauty:

Workers need poetry more than bread. They need that their life should be a poem ... Deprivation of this poetry explains all forms of demoralization. (GG 159)

Weil believed that employers had a responsibility to provide classes for their workers where there would be opportunity to study literature. Her studies of Homer's *Iliad* illustrate the kind of classes she had in mind. More realistically, perhaps, she believed that if workers could be taught to understand some of the basic principles of science, they might better understand the manufacturing process and feel more involved in it. Secondly, if machines were individualized, work might become more satisfying and production rates would consequently increase.

Weil also reflected upon the nature of work, by which she

always meant physical labour in the factory or in the field. Even before her first-hand factory experiences Weil had argued that it was essential that the gap between physical and intellectual labour should be bridged:

The only hope of socialism resides in those who have already brought about in themselves, as far as possible in the society of today, that union between manual and intellectual labour which characterizes the society we are aiming at. (OL 23)

Workers were not given the time nor the education to think, while intellectuals lacked the experience of work. Weil envisioned a working people's culture in which work, science and art would complement one another as equal partners in the task of building society:

Through work [man] produces his own natural existence. Through science he recreates the universe by means of symbols. Through art he recreates the alliance between his body and his soul. (GG 157)

From a Christian perspective, there is nothing unusual about understanding work positively as a sharing in God's creation. George Herbert, the English poet so admired by Weil, had written three centuries earlier:

Who sweeps a room, as for thy laws,
Makes that and the action fine.

But Weil did not believe that work was good because it was a sharing in God's recreation of the world. On the contrary, Weil's experience exposed a flaw in this Christian sentimentalization of work. Herbert had written of 'drudgery divine', yet work as experienced on the factory floor was degrading and filled the soul with disgust. This disgust, Weil argued, had to do with the 'burdensomeness of time' (GG 158). Time, which seems to pass quickly when one is enjoying oneself, or when both hands and mind are occupied, drags on interminably when we are doing something we hate. It is 'effort without finality', for 'Work is like a death if it is without an incentive' (GG 160).

Weil's powerful simile, in contrast with other Christian attitudes to work, makes clear the physical and spiritual cost of work. Work can exhaust body and soul and deprive them of the light of eternity. At this point, it is worth recalling Weil's description of affliction as 'an uprooting of life, a more or less attenuated equivalent of death, made irresistibly present to the soul by the attack or immediate apprehension of physical pain' (WG 62). Both affliction and work are likened to death, affecting body and soul together. But these are not the only similarities between them. Even though work, like affliction, is abhorrent, when we submit to its necessity, it can be a gateway to God. Through work, Weil believes, a human person can learn the hard lesson of obedience to the necessity of the world:

Manual labour. Time entering the body. Through work man turns himself into matter, as Christ does through the Eucharist. Work is like a death.

We have to pass through death. We have to be killed – to endure the weight of the world. When the universe is weighing upon the back of a human creature, what is there to be surprised at if it hurts him?...

To work – if we are worn out it means that we are becoming submissive to time as matter is. Thought is forced to pass from one instant to the next without laying hold of the past or the future. That is what it means to obey. (GG 160)

In this way, Weil argues that the most important characteristic of work is not the way it enables a human person to participate in the *recreation* of the world, as Christian theology had previously suggested, but the way it enables a person to *decreate* herself. By submitting oneself to work, to the burden of time, the ego is dissolved and a vacant space opened to the love of God: 'by fatigue, affliction and death, man is made matter and is consumed by God' (GG 29–30). To Weil, work is one of the most atrocious experiences, but also potentially one of the most beautiful.

Weil's personal experience of work lends tremendous power to her reflections. The practical suggestions she makes to ameliorate these effects should be treated with the utmost respect. However, in her theological reflections on work it is possible to detect a troublesome contradiction. On the one hand, Weil recognizes the degrading effects of work and the way it disgusts the soul; factory life is dehumanizing and everything must be done to improve its conditions. On the other hand, she argues that work is to be submitted to, for fatigue is a means of taking into one's body the burden of time, of decreating the self – it is a gateway to God. Workers, indeed, are peculiarly privileged, since the dehumanizing effect of work also removes any barrier between God and the worker, stripping them of all that is superfluous. Weil's social concern conflicts with her theological valuation of work as a way to God. She solves this dilemma by means of the notion of contradiction:

> All true good carries with it conditions which are contradictory and as a consequence is impossible. He who keeps his attention really fixed on this impossibility and acts will do what is good. In the same way all truth contains a contradiction. Contradiction is the point of the pyramid. (GG 89)

To Weil, *both* the horror *and* the beauty of work are true, and their apparent contradiction is a sign of their truth. Such a solution, however, is effective only in the context of religious faith; in the realm of philosophy the contradiction remains insoluble. Weil's primary achievement in relation to work, nonetheless, is to place it in a position of central importance:

It is not difficult to define the place that spiritual labour should occupy in a well-ordered social life. It should be its spiritual core. (NR 288)

What Makes a Person Sacred?

In 1943, while working for the Free French in London, Weil returned to social and political themes. In several essays she proceeded far beyond her interests in Marxism and work, towards an exploration of the fundamental needs of human beings. In the contemporary political debates of Western countries, one of the concepts most frequently resorted to is that of 'human rights'. In 1948, the countries of the United Nations agreed a 'Universal Declaration of Human Rights', a charter of civil and political rights essential to all individuals. It included the rights to education, to equality before the law, freedom of religion and the right to life. The principle of basic human rights, within Western culture at least, continues to be central to our understanding of good and bad, right and wrong.

To Simone Weil, however, to make human rights the basis of culture is to commit a grave error:

The notion of rights, which was launched into the world in 1789, has proved unable, because of its intrinsic inadequacy, to fulfil the role assigned to it. (SE 10)

The first reason that the notion of human rights has failed, Weil argues, is because it is itself based upon a fundamental misconception of what it is about human beings that is sacred and inviolable. Proponents of human rights believe that the most valuable aspect of a human being is that part of them which is unique, their 'person', or their 'personality'. In her essay on 'Human Personality', however, Weil argues that: 'There is something sacred in every man, but it is not his person. Nor yet is it the human personality' (SE 9). Even our use of language demonstrates this point. We cannot, for example, say to someone 'You do not interest me' without offending against justice. But, Weil argues, it is not in the least offensive to say to someone 'Your person does not interest me': the *real* me, and the *real* you lie deeper than in the outward trappings of 'person' and 'personality'.

Initially, the distinctions Weil makes between person/personality and the sacred in each human being seem like word games. Weil uses an illustration to clarify her point. She imagines meeting a passer-by in the street. His appearance is distinctive, but it is not this that is important, nor is it some hidden inner part of him, his distinctive 'personality'. If it is some hidden inner 'soul' that is sacred, what is to stop someone from poking out his eyes, since even blinded, he still has as much *personality* as he had before? In this way, she argues, the limitations of the concept of personality are laid bare.

It is impossible to define what is meant by respect for human personality. It is not just that it cannot be defined in words. That can be said of many perfectly clear ideas. But this one cannot be conceived either ... (SE 9–10)

If it is not the person or personality in each human being that is sacred, what is it? Weil answers that in her example what is sacred in the passer-by 'is this man; no more and no less ... It is he. The whole of him. The arms, the eyes, the thoughts, everything' (SE 9).

Though it is the whole of the man that is sacred, however, he is not sacred in every respect. It is not because he happens to have blue eyes, or because he has particularly wonderful thoughts that he is sacred; nor is it some aspect of his person, for example that he is famous. His significance is the same if he is a dustman or a duke. What is sacred in this man, Weil concludes, is that if she puts out his eyes 'his soul would be lacerated by the thought that harm was being done to him' (SE 10). However, what would cause the soul to be hurt would not merely be a sense of *personal* injury being done to the body, but rather a sense that a universal injustice was being done. In other words, Weil suggests,

> *When the infliction of evil provokes a cry of sorrowful surprise from the depth of the soul, it is not a personal thing ... It is always, in the last of men as in Christ himself, an impersonal protest.* (SE 12)

Weil believed that deep within each person's heart there is a germ of perfect good that has its origin in God. Such pure good is only present in individuals and society in imperceptible quantities, but like the grain of mustard seed, or the hidden pearl of Jesus' parables, its effects are far-reaching. There is nothing sacred in a person except this grain of perfect goodness, and perfection is by its very nature impersonal. Thus, 'far from its being his person, what is sacred in a human being is the impersonal in him. Everything which is impersonal in man is sacred, and nothing else' (SE 13). In science it is truth that is sacred; in art it is beauty; in people and in society it is the germ of perfect good.

This complex argument may seem to make little difference to the success or failure of the notion of human rights. But, Weil argues, when an appeal is made to the human rights of the individual, it is the rights of the person or personality that are being claimed, and not the deeper, more fundamental needs of the impersonal soul.

> *The notion of rights is linked with the notion of sharing out, of exchange, of measured quantity. It has a commercial flavour, essentially evocative of legal claims and arguments. Rights are always asserted in a tone of contention; and when this tone is adopted, it must rely upon force in the background, or else it will be laughed at.* (SE 18)

Rights are characterized by the desire to claim something from individuals or from society. In contrast, obligations are characterized by the imperative to give something. One result of this is that

'To place the notion of rights at the centre of social conflicts is to inhibit any possible impulse of charity on both sides' (SE 21). Weil is not arguing that rights are bad, nor is she suggesting that personality is bad or unimportant. Weil argues simply that obligations come first:

> *The notion of obligations comes before that of rights, which is subordinate and relative to the former. A right is not effectual by itself, but only in relation to the obligation to which it corresponds.* (NR 3)

While the germ of good, the source of the sacred in every human person, has a supernatural origin, the personality, and the rights associated with it, has its origins in the natural world. To this useful but secular sphere, Weil allocates rights, personality and democracy. In some limited sense, such notions have a role to play. Although the personal and the impersonal are in some respects opposed to one another, one can lead to the other, and thinking about rights can lead one towards the higher goods of truth, justice and compassion. However, as founding blocks of human life and society, these earthly notions on their own are very unreliable. Weil points out that we sometimes criticize people for pushing themselves (their *person*) forward; it is possible to speak of an *abuse* of democracy – Hitler was *elected* to office. Speaking of rights as though they are possessions implies that we can put them to both good and bad uses. In stark contrast at all times and in all places it is *good* to fulfil an obligation: 'Truth, beauty, justice, compassion are always and everywhere good' (SE 24).

For Weil, this curious argument about words (which suffers badly in translation from French to English) demonstrates that only supernatural good is effective in providing 'an armour for the afflicted'. There is, she points out: 'no guarantee for democracy, or for the protection of the person against the collectivity, without a disposition of public life relating it to the higher good which is impersonal and unrelated to any political form' (SE 34).

In her 'Draft for a Statement of Human Obligations' (SE 219–227), and in the first part of *The Need for Roots*, Weil spells out what it means to live as though the higher 'reality is the sole foundation of the good'. Even though this higher reality is beyond the reach of human faculties, men and women can choose to turn their attention towards this good and make it the real goal of their lives. Far from being an activity that leads to a neglect of obligations in this world, attention to the higher good 'is the only possible motive for universal respect towards human beings' (SE 220).

All people are different, and our natural instinct is therefore to respect some people more than others. However, argues Weil, if what we respect in others is the *impersonal* link that every person has to the higher good, then we learn to respect everyone equally irrespective of creed, race, or social status. Because pure good is inaccessible to human perception, expressing respect for the impersonal can only be done indirectly, by recognizing the obligation all people have to respect the needs of the soul and the body in this world. Needs and obligations are closely linked:

> *The possibility of indirect expression of respect for the human being is the basis of obligation. Obligation is concerned with the needs in this world of the souls and bodies of human beings, whoever they may be. For each need there is a corresponding obligation; for each obligation a corresponding need.* (SE 221–2)

The needs of the body are very clear: food, warmth, sleep, health, rest, exercise and fresh air. The needs of the soul are more difficult to enumerate and explain, and it is difficult to compile a complete list. There are, consequently, some differences between the list of the needs of the soul drawn up in her 'Draft for a Statement of Human Obligations' and that in *The Need for Roots*. For example 'privacy' and 'social life' appear in the former, though not in the latter. Nevertheless, the principles remain the same. In her 'Draft for a Statement of Human Obligations' Weil lists the soul's needs in 'pairs of opposites which balance and complete one another' (SE 224). Examples of these are the needs of the soul for equality and hierarchy; for consented obedience and liberty; for truth and of freedom of expression. For each pair of opposites, Weil offers a brief commentary. Concerning equality and hierarchy she writes:

Equality is the public recognition, effectively expressed in institutions and manners, of the principle that an equal degree of attention is due to the needs of all human beings. Hierarchy is the scale of responsibilities. Since attention is inclined to direct itself upwards and remain fixed, special provisions are necessary to ensure the effective comparability of equality and hierarchy. (SE 224)

In *The Need for Roots*, Weil offers fuller explanations of the needs of the soul as examples of the kinds of investigations governments need to undertake if they are to avoid acting sporadically and at random. In subsequent sections Weil explores more deeply the experience of uprootedness. She also proposes examples of natural environments which need to be created for new roots to be grown:

To be rooted is perhaps the most important and least recognized need of the human soul. It is one of the hardest to define. A human being has roots by virtue of his real, active and natural participation in the life of a community which preserves in living shape certain particular treasures of the past and certain particular expectations of the future. (NR 41)

In the period leading up to the Second World War, and more so following France's surrender, people had experienced uprootedness in town, countryside, and in their nation. Weil argued that in order to set down roots, the soul would need new and healthy environments: people need to take root in a country; in a place where their language is spoken and in which there is a shared cultural and historical heritage; in a professional milieu, and in a local neighbourhood.

One example of such an environment is the nation. Weil recognized that 'there is no other way of defining the word nation than as a territorial aggregate whose various parts recognize the authority of the same State' (NR 95). But she also knew that there were limitations to this definition. One limitation was that, especially in times of war, people make the nation an absolute moral value. Others are hated purely because they do not belong to *my* nation. However, Weil argued, 'To posit one's country as an absolute value that cannot be defiled by evil is manifestly absurd' (NR 125). Nationalism does not mean having pride in one's country to the extent that it dissolves all other moral values. To love one's country means, rather, to have compassion for its needs; not to love it for its glory, but to love all within it that can be destroyed 'and is all the more precious on that account' (NR 164). To love one's country in this way illustrates what it means to have set down roots, and shows the damage done by being uprooted from this precious natural environment.

Weil understood that to express respect for human needs in a constitution, in laws, and in the life of a nation was a formidable task. 'Four obstacles,' she wrote,

> *separate us from a form of civilization likely to be worth something: our false conception of greatness; the degradation of the sentiment of justice; our idolization of money; and our lack of religious inspiration.*
> (NR 209)

Plato's Cave

In the essays she wrote in London in 1943, Weil put into the concrete form of ethical proposals the more abstract reflections of her earlier theology. Themes developed during her time in Marseilles, such as her concept of the good or of attention, are applied in these essays to the concrete problem of shaping society in postwar France. De Gaulle may have consigned these essays to the waste-paper basket, but they are amongst Weil's most enduring achievements. However, one idea that lies behind each of these essays needs to be brought into the open.

Weil's reflections on the sacred good latent within the individual, on obligations and on the needs of the soul, have their origin in her love for the philosophy of Plato. In order to understand her ideas, it is helpful to recall one of the key images in Plato's *Republic*. Plato compares our life in the world to a number of men confined to living in a cave since childhood, their feet and necks bound by heavy chains which oblige them to face the back wall of the cave. Behind them lies the cave's entrance, but because of their chains no one in the cave has ever been able to look round to see the sunlit entrance of the cave leading to the outside world. Within the cave, however, runs a low wall behind which is a huge fire. Between the fire and the wall, walk a number of people. They themselves are hidden, but they carry on their shoulders all sorts of statues of people and animals which cast moving shadows onto the wall that the men in chains are facing. In their ignorance of the outside world the men in chains believe that the shadows are real; they even give names to the moving shadows. This shadow life goes on until, by some freak of fate, one of the chained men becomes free. Some unknown force drags the liberated prisoner unwillingly towards the outside light. After the pain of re-focusing his eyes in the dazzling brilliance of sunlight, he sees the real world, and finally learns that all the things he once thought real were actually poor shadows of reality. Returning to the cave the man tries to explain to his companions that their whole world is nothing but dim flickering shadows of reality. No one believes him, he is a laughing-stock, and when he offers to set his companions free, they respond with incredulity, anger and fear.

Plato's story of the cave is, to Weil, a parable of the relationship of this earthly world to the higher reality of the supernatural world. Sure enough, the shadowy world of democracy, personality and human rights bears some relationship to the true light of the supernatural world. The cave is the world, and the chains are our impoverished imaginations. Nevertheless, Plato's parable teaches that we are terribly deceived if we do not make the painful journey into the light of day, where truth, beauty, compassion and the good are more real than anything we can imagine. Only the wise ever make the journey to this higher reality, but then 'The wise have to return to the cave, and act there' (LP 221). They must struggle against incredulity and fear until they 'reach the stage where power is in the hands of those who refuse it, and not of those whose ambition is to possess it' (LP 221).

Neither Plato nor Simone Weil claimed to possess the whole truth about the world, but both believed that the task of the philosopher was to lead others out of the cave. Weil's ideas about the ways in which individuals and societies grow roots have never been taken very seriously. It is as though legislators, politicians, moralists, and the majority of people, are living the whole of their lives in a cave, foolishly satisfied with shadowy realities.

Modern thinkers – philosophers and theologians amongst them – have struggled with the idea that Plato's parable represents the true nature of our situation. There is, according to their counter-argument, no higher reality at all, or if there is, then we have no way of experiencing life outside the cave. We must get used to the unpalatable fact that we have only shadows to look at. This is not as bad, they say, as Weil makes out. Her dream of a higher light only serves to distract attention from the reality, and to devalue the beauty and truth of the world in front of us.

Many components of Weil's essays on human personality, human obligations and the needs of the soul have value irrespective of whether or not we accept her description of reality as split between earthly and higher realities. Her essays can be read as masterpieces of humanist values, admirable in their dogged idealism. Nevertheless, Weil presents us with an unavoidable choice: do we agree or disagree with her that 'There is a reality outside the world, that is to say, outside space and time, outside man's mental universe, outside any sphere whatsoever accessible to human faculties ... [and] just as the reality of this world is the sole foundation of facts, so that other reality is the sole foundation of the good' (SE 219)?

Conclusion

Simone Weil was thirty-four years old when she died. It is disheartening to ponder how much was lost by her tragically early death. What new insights might she have developed? What fresh perspectives might she have offered on the Christian tradition? Such questions are disheartening, but they are also fruitless. Simone Weil must be assessed according to two criteria: the integration of her thought and her actions, and the *truth* of what she wrote.

Weil's first achievement was that her writing grew out of her personal experience. Her debilitating headaches and physical frailty afforded her profound insight into the meaning of affliction. Her mystical experiences formed the raw material on which her creative mind worked to develop an account of the love of God. Her experiences as a factory worker and as a refugee from the Nazis motivated her to explore the value of work and the need for roots. Her experience led to ideas, and she struggled then to put her ideas back into practice. Weil argued forcefully that society has divorced physical labour from intellectual activity at its peril. Weil's life provides us with a model of how valuable can be the results when hand and brain work together. Weil is at her best in *The Need for Roots*, when her experience of physical labour and her insight into the realities of human needs combine to offer a vision for society based on obligations not rights. Her list of the needs of the soul and of the body, as compelling as they are original, have never yet been properly considered by politicians or legislators. The questions raised by Weil challenge the foundations of our society. Being critical of society is one thing, but Weil goes further: in *The Need for Roots* she offers alternative foundations which, if taken seriously, could be used as the basis of a society that might be more just and decent.

Yet there is another side to the way in which Weil integrated thought and life. If we are prepared to believe that her thought may be somehow authenticated by the way it was integrated with her life, we must also be prepared to accept that her life may show up limitations in her thought. Weil insisted repeatedly that suffering must never be sought, while affliction must be embraced whenever it comes as a way of encounter with God. In fairness she also argued that joy was a gateway to God. The vital thing about both joy and affliction is that they must be accepted in their purest forms. Nevertheless, Weil undeniably put herself in the way of suffering. She laboured in factories when she was physically unsuited to the work, she sought danger in Spain, she became dispirited with the Free French because they would not give her a dangerous mission, and she went to the extraordinary extent of envying those who were paralysed. Even in more mundane matters, such as food and dress, she almost made a point of despising her bodily needs, which were always subordinated to her spiritual needs.

The lack of personal integration between spirit and body in Weil raises important questions about the relationship between physical and spiritual reality in her theology. Detachment, acceptance of the void, decreation, self-effacement: do these themes tally properly with the theology of the incarnation of God in Christ?

'This world is the closed door,' wrote Weil. 'It is a barrier. And at the same time it is the way through' (GG 132). '...God crosses through the thickness of the world to come to us' (GG 82). Attachment to the world is an illusion, for reality is found beyond the world. A theology of the incarnation, however, suggests that God's reality is indeed to be found within the physical reality of this world, in bread and wine, and above all in the physical presence of

God in Jesus. Weil's theology has at its centre the concept that there is a reality beyond the physical reality of this world, and that this higher reality is to be a person's true goal. Readers of Weil must ask if this encourages or discourages human beings to engage in the concrete mundane struggles of daily life.

This leads us to what Weil herself regarded as the most important question about her thought: its truth. Weil wrote: 'The eulogies of my intelligence are positively *intended* to evade the question: "Is what she says true?"'

It is not an easy question to answer. For most of us, poised at the turn of the century, truth is an uncomfortable concept. Professional theologians and ethicists have become increasingly sceptical about making dogmatic claims. Originally, dogma meant simply a system of beliefs, but now dogma has become a dirty word, and someone who is dogmatic is thought of as intolerant of other points of view. Weil's notion of truth is not a traditional one. She learned from Marx, but rejected the unquestioning dogma of the Marxists. She regarded herself as a Christian, but refused baptism because she could not subscribe to the whole of Roman Catholic dogma. In spite of her rejection of dogma in other systems, Weil made dogmatic claims of her own. Weil believed that there were strands of divine truth that ran through many religious and philosophical traditions. She argued that the presence of the same religious beliefs in different traditions meant that they must be true. One such religious truth was God's suffering. Thus, Weil draws parallels between the truth contained in the ancient Greek myth of the suffering of Prometheus and the suffering of Christ:

'My God, my God, why has thou forsaken me?' There we have the real proof that Christianity is something divine. (GG 79)

But why should suffering be a true mark of God while, say, the idea that God is not susceptible to pain and suffering (a concept philosophers and theologians call divine impassibility) is false?

The impassibility of God is found in several religious traditions, in Greek thought, in some Buddhist traditions, and in Christian theology, but Weil rejects it in favour of suffering as a defining characteristic of God. On what grounds, other than her assertion that it is so, are we to know that suffering, and not impassibility is characteristic of God's relationship to the world?

This is only one example, but there are other instances in which Weil asserts that something is true, but fails to show why it is true. Weil's repeated insistence that one should seek what is true in her writings begs the question about what truth is. Weil claims that we must seek truth, but is she right to assume that recognizing 'truth' is as straightforward for the rest of us as it was for her?

The question 'What is truth?' is not the most interesting or fruitful subject in Weil's writings. The only reason it attracts attention is that Weil so explicitly made the question of truth the rod by which to measure her achievements. If we are to look for more lasting achievements, Weil's examination of God's existence or nonexistence, or her theology of affliction, are much more interesting and imaginative.

The greater part of this book has been taken up with simply presenting Weil's thought with a minimum of critical comment or analysis. However, the aim has not been to present Weil's thought as though she was a saint whose writings should be accepted without criticism. The questions raised here and in earlier chapters about aspects of Weil's thought are only a small proportion of the difficulties careful readers will find themselves struggling with in her writings. However, although 'truth' was the criterion Weil asked to be judged by, also important is her unerring ability to get to the heart of some of the key philosophical, theological and ethical issues of our time. Thus, though readers may not always agree with what Weil proposes, the impression left by her legacy is overwhelmingly positive. Weil belongs amongst those Christian thinkers who leave aside peripheral issues, and take us instead to the few most important questions about God and about life.

Conclusion

One commentator has noted astutely that writing about Weil is like trying to advertise sunshine. Originality; the ability to strip away the dead wood of traditional theology and to bring fresh life to tired doctrines; courage in tackling social and political subjects from a Christian perspective – these are Weil's gifts. To dismiss them because Weil fails to fit comfortably into preconceived ideas of Christian theology will result in the impoverishment of us all.

Suggested Further Reading

Books by Simone Weil

Gateway to God, Collins Fontana, 1974. A collection of extracts from some of Weil's most important essays, including those on the love of God, and on the love of God and affliction. One of the best introductions to Weil's thought.

Gravity and Grace, Routledge, 1987. A collection of extracts from Weil's *Notebooks.* This is one of the best books to buy to give you a feel of Weil's thought. It is in the form of short notes on various subjects.

Intimations of Christianity among the Ancient Greeks, Ark Paperbacks, 1987. A selection of Weil's writings on ancient Greek tragedy and philosophy including her essays on Antigone, on Prometheus, and on God in Plato. To read this book some knowledge of ancient Greek thought is helpful.

The Need for Roots, Ark Paperbacks, 1987. This is the longest of Weil's essays. It is concerned primarily with society and is not overtly a theological book.

Waiting for God, HarperCollins, 1973. Extracts from many of Weil's most important essays and, with *Gateway to God,* a good introduction to her thought. It includes her 'Spiritual Biography' and the essay on 'Forms of the Implicit Love of God'.

Books about Simone Weil

Bell, Richard, ed., *Simone Weil's Philosophy of Culture,* Cambridge University Press, 1993. This book is a collection of essays by several commentators examining Weil's thought in much greater depth. It is not an introduction.

McLellan, David, *Simone Weil: Utopian Pessimist,* Papermac (Macmillan), 1989. McLellan mixes Weil's biography with her thought very well. McLellan's speciality is political theory, however, and Weil's theology is not his main interest. Nevertheless, it is an excellent full-length introduction.

Pétrement, Simone, *Simone Weil: A Life,* Pantheon, 1976.

Details of other books by Simone Weil

First and Last Notebooks, Oxford University Press, 1970.

Formative Writings 1929–1941, eds. D. McFarland and W. Van Ness, University of Massachusetts Press, 1987.

Lectures in Philosophy, Cambridge University Press, 1978.

The Notebooks of Simone Weil, 2 vols., Routledge, 1956.

On Science, Necessity and the Love of God, Oxford University Press, 1968.

Oppression and Liberty, University of Massachusetts Press, 1973.

Selected Essays, Oxford University Press, 1962.

Seventy Letters, Oxford University Press, 1965.

Index